Designing for Re-use

Designing for Re-use

The Life of Consumer Packaging

Tom Fisher and Janet Shipton

publishing for a sustainable future

London • Sterling, VA

First published by Earthscan in the UK and USA in 2010

Copyright © Janet Shipton and Tom Fisher, 2010

ISBN: 978-1-84407-487-7   hardback
          978-1-84407-488-4   paperback

Typeset by Safehouse Creative
Cover design by Rob Watts

For a full list of publications please contact:

Earthscan
Dunstan House
14a St Cross Street
London EC1N 8XA, UK
Tel: +44 (0)20 7841 1930
Fax: +44 (0)20 7242 1474
Email: earthinfo@earthscan.co.uk
Web: **www.earthscan.co.uk**

22883 Quicksilver Drive, Sterling, VA 20166-2012, USA

Earthscan publishes in association with the International Institute for Environment and
Development

A catalogue record for this book is available from the British Library

Library of Congress Cataloging-in-Publication Data

Fisher, Tom (Thomas Henry Sutton), 1958-
  Designing for re-use : the life of consumer packaging / Tom Fisher and Janet Shipton. -- 1st
ed.
    p. cm.
  Includes bibliographical references and index.
  ISBN 978-1-84407-487-7 (hardback) -- ISBN 978-1-84407-488-4 (pbk.) 1. Packaging waste--Envi-
ronmental aspects--Great Britain. 2. Packaging--Design--Environmental aspects--Great Britain.
3. Salvage (Waste, etc.)--Citizen participation--Great Britain. I. Shipton, Janet. II. Title. III. Title:
Life of consumer packaging.

  TD797.9.F57 2010
  688.8028'6--dc22
                              2009031296

Contents

List of Figures

Introduction

The list to the right contains things that people have done with the packaging[1] they encounter in their everyday lives – re-using it. Some of them are one-offs, where someone solves a problem around the house with a leftover piece of packaging, but for others packaging is standing in for items that would otherwise have to be bought specially for the purpose. Some of the former are perhaps engaging, but only as examples of everyday inventiveness, and therefore no more than curiosities. The latter, on the other hand, should interest us, because in such cases, by being re-used, a piece of apparently valueless waste has gained the value of an item someone would otherwise have to buy.

It is normal to think of packaging as having no value once it has done its job. Although it may be possible to recycle its material, often it has to be thrown away; it gets wasted, posing a problem of how to get rid of it. Re-using a piece of apparently worthless packaging means getting value from it at no cost, and if it is substituting for an item that would have to be bought it is possible to quantify that value. Each carrier bag re-used as a bin bag saves x pence against the bin bags I would have otherwise bought. Because re-used packaging gains the value of the item it substitutes for, it avoids the re-user incurring that cost. That makes re-use attractive in terms of the economics of individual households, but there are collective benefits to this cost-saving. The object that re-used packaging substitutes for would carry the environmental cost that any manufactured item has in material, manufacture and transport. When a person substitutes a piece of packaging for an item they not only avoid incurring an economic cost to themselves, but also avoid incurring an environmental cost to us all.

Packaging waste is well known to cause people a good deal of concern.[2] It regularly gets in the news and because it is so visible, both in the environment

fifty-five gallon drum as chair • beer can as camping stove • beer cans as barometer • blue wine bottles for decorative display • can/bottle as shallow dish • cardboard as material for furniture • cardboard box as stationery cupboard • cardboard boxes as storage • carrier bag as rucksack • carrier bags as bin liners • carrier bags as dog poo bags • carrier bags for garden equipment protection • carrier bags reused as bags • cd packaging as flower pot • cereal packets for stencils • champagne box as light • coffee cups as plant pots • coffee jars

and in our waste bins; it seems sometimes to be the focus for a more generalized anxiety about the risks we run as a result of the effects our way of life may have on the environment. We have mixed feelings about it; we buy prepared food, presumably because we want it and like it, but some of us feel bad about the packaging that comes along with it and ends up as bulky waste, which we can't always recycle to make ourselves feel better.[3]

Such feelings may be what motivates some people to re-use packaging where they can. While it is not possible to quantify the impact of re-use on resource consumption, it is possible to delineate its features. Some of it is remarkably inventive – people with no particular qualifications apply significant creativity in finding ways to reuse packaging, and this makes them feel good, so good in fact that they are often keen to share their ideas online. These are not people who are coming up with creative designs for re-used packaging as part of their professional life, creating products which can then be capitalized on by being sold; these are people simply identifying a nifty thing you can do with something that would otherwise be waste. Sharing such ideas seems to be part of the satisfaction it is possible to get from them. It was such indigenous creative re-use that inspired this book. Although we, the authors, both come from a design background – Janet has worked as a packaging designer for nearly 20 years and Tom has done a good deal of consumer research related to packaging – it was clear to us that this spontaneous packaging re-use is an under-researched phenomenon, and that it may be possible to think of packaging as a resource rather than a problem.

This book is about how to understand the re-use that goes on in people's homes, to better understand how this resource might be capitalized on in the future. A first step in this direction is to think about what the term 'packaging re-use' refers to – over and above the particular examples listed above. It has a strong relationship to use in that it is part of people's whole relationship to material goods – anything

for paintbrush soaking and storage • coke bottles as display • coke cans for halloween cape • crate 'upcycled' with silver bubble wrap • crisp packet as pencil case • decorative metal tin for sewing needle storage • designer shoebox for photo storage • detergent bottle as worm harvester • drink concentrate container as water butt • duty-free metal tin as seed packet container • fish tin as desk tidy • glass jam jars for herbs and spices storage • glass jar for diy part storage • glass jars for cotton wool ear bud storage • glass jars to hold bath crystals • ice-cream tubs for plant pots • ice-cream containers

can be re-used for a purpose other than that it was intended to fulfil, with more or less adaptation. Buildings, furniture, clothes, urban environments, implements, vehicles – all these are re-used, and the design of some of them makes their re-use easier, the modular construction of steel and concrete architecture being an example. Re-use means employing an object for something other than its original purpose – re-use for something else, or as something else. Re-use is a conventional aspect of our relationship to material goods. However, re-use also goes against the grain of a type of object which we assume will be consumed by being 'used up', with no usefulness left over that can be capitalized on; packaging could be the defining example of this type of consumption. The fact that packaging *is* re-used means that the part it plays in our lives actually has more in common with other things we 'consume' without physically using up, using them to play out our identities.

Packaging re-use is not only little understood, it is misunderstood. Many people assume it is the same as recycling packaging materials to make them into something else by re-processing them, melting glass, metal and plastic to make them into new material for new products, for example. As the list of examples of re-use here shows, this is not what this book is about. There is a relationship between some of the examples in the book and what McDonough and Braungart (2003) call 'upcycling' – using objects as material for something that is as useful or more useful than the original. Some of the examples do treat packaging as a source of material, but without re-processing it through recycling. However, the re-uses of packaging in this book that use packaging as a source of material do not have the normal characteristics of upcycling, which is usually done in an industrial setting, small or large, with the resulting items being for sale. This book concentrates on the life of consumer packaging in consumers' homes.

The UK Government recognizes the potential for packaging to be more frequently and extensively re-used; however it demonstrates a restricted view

for small toy part storage • ice-cream plastic container for pet food storage • inverted plastic bottles used as bird-scarers • kilner jars for various storage • metal biscuit tin as a first-aid box • metal round tin for storage • metal tins for decoration in pubs • metal toffee tin for diy bits storage • milk container as wasp trap • oil tin as spice shelf • paper cups as pencil holders • pasta sauce containers for freezing food • pizza boxes as seed trays • plastic (zip lock) bags for ice • plastic two-litre milk carton as a garden scoop • plastic two-litre water bottle as a cloche • plastic bags as material to make a hoodie

of what this potential consists of. A recent report by Defra (2009) tells of the progress that has been made to reduce the environmental impact of packaging. It outlines the successes of the UK Government in promoting recycling – 60 per cent is now recycled, up from 28 per cent in 1997 – and the principles for minimizing the impact of packaging through design by, for instance, reducing its weight. The short section of the report on re-use raises the reader's hopes that the UK Government understands something of the potential that exists for consumers' actions to ameliorate the environmental impact of packaging, but this promise is not fulfilled. The report notes that the re-use of containers in 'closed loops' – where a container is returned to the manufacturer for re-filling – is now quite rare, but its authors appear to assume that this is the only way packaging can be re-used. The examples the report gives are not in the closed-loop category. It describes packs for soap and cleaning fluids that have a spray or pump dispenser for which it is possible to buy refills. While this means that the pump might be reused, the empty container is still designed to be discarded rather than being returned and re-filled.

The UK's success in reducing the impact of packaging has derived from a market-orientated approach to the problem, enlisting the support of manufacturers and retailers. Consumers are involved in this approach to the extent that they make up markets for packaged goods, and manufacturers, retailers and government are sensitive to their views on which aspects of the problem of packaging are most significant to them. However, characterizing our relationship to the environmental impact of packaging as simply caught in a conflict between desire for packaged goods and distaste for waste underplays the potential that exists to ameliorate the negative effects of packaging by taking advantage of some of the things that people actually do with it, particularly how they re-use it. This book starts with the premise that it is possible to increase the impact of this spontaneous creativity with packaging by an approach to design that works with

• plastic bags as stuffing for decoy bird • plastic bags remade as decorative flowers • plastic biscuit box as storage • plastic carrier bags for weed collection, handing storage, etc • plastic dog food container as laundry basket • plastic drink bottle as bird feeder • plastic drink bottle as biscuit cutter • plastic drink bottle as building brick • plastic drink bottle as butter churn • plastic drink bottle as cable holder • plastic drink bottle as chicken waterer • plastic drink bottle as cistern water saver • plastic drink bottle as coin purse • plastic drink bottle as electric fence insulator • plastic drink

it. This approach to designing does more than simply include consumers in a design process located in the professional sphere of production by recognizing their desires and opinions: it engages fully with what people already do with packaging in everyday life as both a starting point for design and as a force that is independent of the system of production and that has the potential to change our relationship to packaging by influencing that system. At the level of the design of packaging, one element of this approach is to recognize the importance of not closing off potential ways to re-use it, aiming for 'open' rather than 'closed' designs. 'Open' objects have re-use potential because they have many potential uses, most of which will not be known to the designer because they depend on being found by inventive consumers. They emerge out of the ways that people relate to packaging in their everyday circumstances, rather than being imposed on the object through its design. They are so tightly tied into the practices of everyday life it is not possible to design *for* them. The design of packaging can facilitate reuse, leaving openings for it, but it can also close off possibilities for people to integrate packaging into their lives in ways not foreseen by its designers. A bottle that is designed to be re-used as a brick may only ever be re-used as a brick.

In its orientation towards the future, this type of design process is in sympathy with the aspects of UK government efforts that do recognize the significance of how people integrate packaging into their everyday lives. Defra's report of 2009 outlines three possible future scenarios for packaging, one of which, titled 'values shift', opens up the possibility that over the next ten years waste will come to be seen as a resource, as well as a greater emphasis being put on 'repair and re-use as well as community sharing and home production of food and other goods'. While this vision may contain as much idealism as realism given the apparent lack of power that values seem to have against the forces that entrench the habits and systems that generate packaging waste, it is

bottle as fish/bee trap • plastic drink bottle as freezer thermal mass • plastic drink bottle as heat-shrink • plastic drink bottle as light shade for fluorescent lamps • plastic drink bottle as mobile speaker enclosure • plastic drink bottle as mouse/rat trap • plastic drink bottle as pen holder • plastic drink bottle as phytoplankton culture container • plastic drink bottle as piggy bank • plastic drink bottle as pool chlorinator • plastic drink bottle as prosthetic arm • plastic drink bottle as rubber band-powered toy • plastic drink bottle as scoop • plastic drink bottle as small items organizer

encouraging to see the relationship made between values and what people do with packaging. However, there is little sense in this of the potential that exists for the things that people do spontaneously with packaging to be the starting point for a changed collective relationship with it. These ways of re-using packaging are largely independent of the system of provision, other than the fact that the system provides their raw material. They exist in parallel to it and demonstrate an alternative way of consumers relating to packaging by thinking of it as a resource that can be useful to them, rather than as a problem that needs to be got rid of or for others to deal with.

Familiar ways of thinking about how people and packaging interact pay attention to only some aspects of the relationship. People are assumed to have power, as consumers making choices about what to buy, choices that may be influenced both by their experiences as users – they want packs to open easily and perform adequately – and by the advertising signals the pack gives them about how the product might relate to their ideas about themselves. Similarly, people relate to packaging as citizens, conforming more or less to injunctions from government and the influence of collective opinion about how to dispose of waste packaging properly to allow its material to be recycled. Behind this is an image of a flow of material that is turned into packaging by manufacturers, is briefly put to use by people in their homes, and then arrives in the hands of agencies that recycle its material to manufacture or reclaim energy from it. This progress of packaging from production to waste-stream has the sense of an inevitable flow, as if determined by the natural force of gravity, a rational, tidy, predictable and therefore manageable flow. However, the fact that the life that consumer packaging may have between production and waste is absent from this analogy means it ignores an important element in the way packaging actually moves through our homes in its journey from factory to garbage. Our experience of shared spaces tells us that packaging is actually unruly – it doesn't

• plastic drink bottle as storage container • plastic drink bottle as table lamp • plastic drink bottle as thermos • plastic drink bottle as toilet-mounted bean sprouter • plastic drink bottle as vase • plastic drink bottle caps as basket • plastic drink bottle for indoor disc golf • plastic drink bottles as buoy • plastic drink bottles as drinking cups • plastic drink bottles as hydroponics system • plastic drink bottles as roof insulation • plastic drink bottles as upside-down hanging planters • plastic drink bottles for aquaculture photo-bioreactor • plastic film pots for buttons •

flow neatly and often ends up as litter. In a similar way, in our homes, as this book shows, although it sometimes behaves like a well-channelled fluid, an organized stream, it also sloshes about, spills, forms pools and collects in puddles in inconvenient places, or reappears having been dammed up in a back-water for a while. And this fluid analogy breaks down completely when we think about how water may disappear by evaporation, or by sinking conveniently into the ground; packaging does neither.

This book is about diversions to the normal flow of packaging, the puddles and backwaters rather than the well-ordered stream. Some of these diversions mean that packaging ends up serving some purpose or other that its designers cannot, by definition, have predicted, because they have been figured out by people as they deal with its steady trickle through their homes. Is this open-loop re-use? It is certainly very different from closed-loop re-use, but it is not necessarily a loop at all, rather a temporary diver-sion of the flow that has benefits in the consumption that it replaces. One thing serves two purposes. The following chapters show how packaging sometimes lingers in people's homes and how what happens to it, what it does and what is done to it, results from a rich set of relationships between human agents and packaging objects in a process of evolution, stimu-lated and supported by communication online. This last is explored in the final chapter, but suggests itself as the most convincing mechanism to bring about the necessary change in values that would need to accompany changes to the way we live with pack-aging to involve more re-use. But values are only part of the picture – people do creative things to re-use the physical properties that they find built into pack-aging in particular spaces – houses, gardens, sheds, allotments. They have particular feelings about what is appropriate to do that are built into everyday habits and routines. All the elements of this system need to adjust to facilitate re-use; it is not possible to understand, or to change, the whole system by concentrating only on one of its parts.

plastic film pots for seed storage • plastic lidded food containers as wool holders • plastic sweets tub for various storage • plastic milk bottles made into watering can • plastic pots as saucers • plastic takeaway carton for freezing food • plastic take-away container as lunchbox • plastic trays for fruit and veg storage • plastic water bottles made into christmas fairy • polystyrene cups broken down and made into plant pot drainage filler • pot noodle containers for plant pots • ready-mix cement bucket for further diy use • ring-pulls as bag • ring-pulls as dress • shoe-box inside-out to show

Notes

1   This book takes 'consumer packaging' to indicate those containers and wrappings that people bring home with them from the shops, or that arrive by mail order, that contain the goods we have purchased. These are the bags, boxes, tubs, jars, pouches, cartons and so on that we buy along with the category of purchases known as 'fast-moving consumer goods'. In the packaging industry these are known as 'primary' packs. Shops use secondary packs to display goods on the shelf and receive these in tertiary packs which are used exclusively for transport. We do not normally encounter these types of packaging.
2   People's concerns about packaging – worry about its impact and wastefulness – appear to be balanced for many by the benefits in convenience it brings (Defra, 2009, p9; Incpen, 1997).
3   Each household buys on average 200kg of packaging a year, of which 60 per cent is now recycled (Defra, 2009).

References

Defra (2009) *Making the Most of Packaging: A Strategy for a Low-Carbon Economy*, Department for Environment, Food and Rural Affairs, London

Incpen (The Industry Council for Packaging and the Environment) (1997) 'Consumer attitudes to packaging', available at www.incpen.org/pages/data/Consumerattitudestopackagingsurvey.pdf, last accessed May 2008

McDonough, W. and Braungart, M. (2002) *Cradle to Cradle: Remaking the Way we Make Things*, North Point Press, New York

plain surface • takeaway boxes as dress • tissue paper shredded for packing gifts • toilet roll middles for plant support • washing tablet net bags for toy storage • wine bottles as candle holders • wine box inner bags as material • wooden packing case as storage • yoghurt pot lids as dress • yoghurt pots for cleaning small items • yoghurt pots for craft activity • yoghurt pots for bird feeders • yoghurt pots for freezer storage.

1

History, Habits and Principles: Objects, People and Places

Introduction

Once you become aware of it, you seem to see packaging re-use everywhere you look. Garden trees with yoghurt pots hung from their branches as bird feeders; a plastic carrier bag re-used as a hat; allotment gardeners using drinks bottles to protect plants; your workmate's lunchbox that was a takeaway container. Although the subject may have a tinge of 'waste not want not' frugality and an anti-consumerist flavour, its sheer ubiquity in response to consumerism, and the fact that it is dependent on the modern scale of consumption for its raw material, suggests that what motivates it – how it fits with people's lives and their relationships with the material world in general – is more complex than it might seem. This is not something that only radical environmentalists do. Packaging is raw material for any further use that human creativity can identify, and this includes the most technical uses – it may be that only a small number of people will want to re-use a tin can as part of a computer wireless network antenna, but it is possible to do so (Rehm, 2007).

Packaging is the visible excess of contemporary consumption. It is what is left over, surplus, discarded on the way to the objects that we desire. It provides manufacturers with a set of opportunities – conveniently long shelf-life; engaging surfaces for branding; a way of making a product compete with others on a shelf. And these functions are usually themselves finished, used up, after goods enter the home. It is carefully designed, but designed to have no value, to be disposable, to be waste. Packaging is the 'excess' of consumption; it is ephemeral, but it gets in the way; we need it, but it offends us when it is out of place; we require it but simultaneously are disgusted by it. Attracted by it in the shop, our dislike of packaging seems to operate on two levels. It offends when it is 'matter out of place', when it is used but not hidden, when it is 'dirt' and therefore polluting, when it gets where it shouldn't. It is also a focus for guilt at the scale of contemporary consumption. We buy into an ethic of 'untouched by human hand' (Tomes, 1999; Hooper, 1932) which requires packaging, at the same time as being disgusted by its consequences.

Pondering on things we consider of no value helps us to understand what we do value, and why. The transformation of objects from one state to the other, packaging re-valued, made to coincide with a configuration of useful-ness that contradicts its conventional destiny, may help us to see something of our relationship with other classes of possessions. John Scanlan (2005) notes that the emphasis in recent social and cultural theory on the spectacular aspects of consumption as part of modern material culture means waste has not featured very strongly, though studies do exist of the history of waste (Strasser, 1999; Rogers, 2005) and of the ways in which we deal with unwanted things in our homes (Gregson et al, 2007a and b). This book points towards a shift in our relationship to packaging, made urgent perhaps by the frequent attention that packaging gets in the press as a contemporary evil. If we can put our hand in the bin and take something out that is coherent, that is clean or can be cleaned of the traces of its first use, and it can fill some need or other, we might, we just might, use it again. This is a radical step and people who are in the habit of taking it have to go against the grain of a system that is embedded in our built surroundings and ingrained in our habits and our psyches. Our homes are designed around the packaged products that we bring into them and which appear to flow through them. These products either soon shed their temporary clothing of plastic, cardboard and paper, or are used up and leave an exoskeleton of discarded packaging as an unwelcome trace of their short life. This material is channelled down the household *cloaca*[1] of waste bin and dustbin, to be dealt with by municipal services that we pay for out of our taxes. This system is similarly entrenched in our attitudes and assumptions. It is played out through our feelings about what is and is not acceptable in our physical surroundings, feelings which require the a-septic consumerism that packaging makes possible and make us ready to accept the assumption that the material excess of its leftovers has no value.

Given the strength of these feelings, and the degree to which assumptions about the progress of packaging from shopping bag to bin are entrenched both in our system of provisioning and the arrangement of our homes, it requires some strength of will to disrupt it. People do interrupt the apparently natural flow of packaging by re-using it, however, and the idea behind this book is that by understanding the circumstances in which they do so, it may be possible for design to work with this spontaneous consumer creativity and thereby promote packaging re-use. This implies a particular approach to designing – one that relates to recently developed conventions in design practice and also to the strongly market-orientated tradition of packaging design itself. The 'user-centred' ethic in design has offered a powerful way of developing new technologies that are easy for people to integrate into their lives (Norman, 1990 and 1999). This approach to designing has proved effective with the information and communication technologies that can strongly influence the ways that people work, interact and fill their leisure time.

Developing this type of product brings together a range of disciplines and approaches. Non-designers are prominent in such product-development teams. Social scientists – psychologists, sociologists and anthropologists – may work closely with designers and engineers to originate the product's form and function. The types of research that these teams undertake is also diverse and concentrates on the experiences people will have with the resulting products, going a long way beyond the emphasis on market groups which may be familiar from earlier forms of product-development process (Laurel, 2003). This emphasis on human experience, including feelings both positive and negative that people can have about and with objects (Hirschman and Holbrook, 1982; Holbrook, 1996; Jordan, 1997; Blythe et al, 2003; Fisher, 2004; Desmet and Hekkert, 2002), has led to a reassessment of the concept of 'user-centred' design, criticized as an over-simple and mechanistic approach to people's experience with objects. So Richard Buchanan's emphasis on 'the central place of human beings' in design (2001, p37) has gone along with the emergence of a 'human-centred' ethic which honours the diversity of ways we live with and experience material things and the influence of politics, economics and shared culture on those experiences.

Attempts to integrate the functionalist flavour of user-centred design with the more recent orientation to people's experiences of the designed world – their feelings and emotions – has seen attention turn to the concept of social practice as a basis for designing (Fisher 2008a, Fisher 2008b). This 'practice orientated' approach seeks to pay attention simultaneously to the physicality of our material environment, what is built into it, and to the ways people nego-tiate, adapt, value and form relationships with it (Shove et al, 2007). This view of how designed objects end up 'behaving' with people acknowledges that the physicality of objects influences how people interact with them as well as what they might symbolize. Some writers have emphasized this active role that objects play in our interactions with them – they 'push back' at us (Dant, 1999) – and while the properties they have are put there by us, they also influ-ence us in what we do. In this respect they have a degree of what sociologists call 'agency' (Callon, 1987; Latour, 1992 and 2000) – and this has a role in determining the way we integrate them into our lives, what we think they say about us, how they influence our self-identity, the roles they have in our social relationships and therefore what we can do with them.

Designing that responds to this view of our relationship with objects must work with the patterns of everyday life rather than trying to impose fixed solu-tions to problems, and this is the spirit that motivates this book. The following chapters set out some of the ways that people re-use packaging to show how it 'behaves' in our lives as a result of the combination of what is built into it – its physical properties, the systems of production and consumption into which it is fixed, and the things people do with it. It is the relationship between these three elements – materiality, system and use – that makes packaging what it is, and only by engaging with all three is it possible to understand and influ-ence packaging re-use. It is only possible to design for the ways that people re-use packaging by acknowledging that they do this in very diverse ways, taking advantage of the openings that packaging provides for re-use, which by definition goes against its intended function but in some way or other fits with the pattern of their lives. Designing for re-use therefore requires building openness into packaging, as well as being aware of the ways in which people may take advantage of this openness.

People and Objects: Homes as Waste Processors and Generators

Contemporary homes are like factories processing the products that we buy, preparing them for use and physical consumption by stripping them of their layers of packaging and then contributing to that ubiquitous product of everyday life, waste. Awareness of the waste packaging we throw out stimulates a good deal of anxiety and guilty hand-wringing, which results in headline-grabbing demands to ban carrier bags or to leave packaging at the supermarket. However, relatively little is known about the positive contribution to sustainability that we can make when packaging enters the home but does not leave because we re-use it as a substitute for another purchase. This book describes how, where and when packaging is re-used. It shows that this re-use depends to some extent on physical factors that can be designed into packaging, as well as factors that can be used to make packaging desirable in itself. To oversimplify, there are three aspects to the re-use of packaging: the packaging object itself, where it is and the type of person who is re-using it.

Although packaging appears ephemeral – it is often deliberately designed to be light and insubstantial – the quantity of waste packaging in our collective household 'product' is prodigious. The UK produces ten million tonnes of waste packaging a year, which equates to the weight of a medium sized family car for every three households.[2] Our consumption of packaging becomes starkly obvious at the seasonal peak in our buying as we struggle to close the wheelie bin on the discarded portion of our Christmas binge, or if the system of disposal breaks down when there is a refuse collection strike. This domestic system of 'goods in' and 'waste out' is modified, however, when packaging is re-used in the household. This has consequences for the output side of our domestic factory. The amount of waste produced is reduced, as is the amount of goods entering, if re-used packaging is substituted for a new item.

While there is plenty of information available on the amount of waste we produce, much less is known about the times when people spontaneously re-use packaging that would otherwise go in the bin. As well as trying to work out what motivates people to do this and what types of people are likely to have this motivation, one of the fundamental purposes of this book is to simply show the different ways that consumers re-use packaging. It also shows how this re-use fits with other everyday habits and explains how it fits into the spatial ordering of the home, the 'where and when' of packaging re-use. So it looks into those hidden areas of houses – the cupboards under the sink, the shed, the cellar – to find examples of packaging being re-used and draws on the first-hand testimony of consumers to explain what sort of influences have led them to take this action. Finally, it suggests ways that design can work with what consumers are already doing spontaneously without any guidance and little concrete incentive.

Re-use should be of interest to designers concerned with sustainability, because sustainable consumption does not automatically mean consuming less. As Charter et al (2002) explain, it can mean consuming in a different and 'smarter' way. However, the ways that consumers interact with goods involve many factors, some of them beyond the scope of designers to influence alone. The packaging industry and government's emphasis on recycling or biodegradable materials as solutions to waste management may actually be counter-productive as a long-term approach to waste minimization in that it distances people from direct contact with the problem, lessening their sense of ownership and responsibility for it.

In contrast to the trend for 'instructive' approaches to waste minimization that focus on ways to enforce environmental legislation and pro-environmental consumer behaviour at a macro-level, this book puts the creativity of individual consumers at the centre of the subject in an effort to work with the variety of ways people behave with the detritus of consumption that is packaging. For this reason, even though this book is intended to help designers and manufacturers to encourage packaging re-use through design, it contains as much about the various contexts for re-use as about actual designs or pieces of re-used packaging. It stresses the network of connections – the social mores, the consumer orientations, the domestic arrangements – that influence a decision to re-use a piece of packaging as much as the materials, brand identity and form of the packaging itself.

The life of packaging in the household is relatively invisible, and even though many consumers do re-use packaging, the emphasis on recycling has perhaps contributed to this lack of visibility. The lack of attention to what consumers do with packaging in their homes means consumers and designers often do not understand what packaging re-use is and how it differs from recycling. As a consequence of this lack of understanding, 'recycling' is often used to identify all pro-environmental actions to reduce packaging waste, and for this reason, it is important to define what we mean by 'domestic packaging re-use'.

For our purpose here, 'domestic packaging re-use' is taken to mean the ways consumers re-use the types of 'primary' packaging that survives its designed-in function to promote, protect and help transport goods. While transit packaging such as stretch wrap and film makes up a significant proportion of packaging waste, it does not fall within the scope of this book. It is not generally appropriate for re-use as it usually has no immediately useful form once the product is unwrapped. If it is to be put to another function in the home without being recycled, in other words without being melted down and re-made as a lower grade of plastic, it will need to be processed and re-manufactured to some extent before it can function as a new object. We are not talking about the artful use of packaging materials for what is sometimes known as 'thrift-craft', where something new is made from old materials using low-tech processes. While the results of this sort of activity are engaging, and constitute the re-use of packaging *materials*, the sort of re-use described in this book is more varied, and does not necessarily emphasize the appearance of the resulting useful object, since it is usually carried out relatively privately and not to produce items for sale. Although he was not writing about packaging but about manufactured goods, Victor Corral-Verdugo's definition of re-use is helpful to distinguish it from recycling:

> *Re-use is the use of an object in a different, additional way from that originally intended when the object was purchased. In re-use, objects are neither discarded nor reprocessed, but keep their original form. The only thing that changes is their use or the person using them.* (1996, p 666)

What we are talking about here is the re-use of packaging that remains 'coherent' after it has done the job it was designed for and which can be re-used more or less as it is, or with some modification.[3] Later chapters show that re-use of this sort of packaging is common and is carried out by many types of people for sometimes quite individual reasons. This is re-use activity that is spontaneous, sometimes inventive, sometimes artful but not necessarily systematic or planned. At its extremes, people may re-use a piece of packaging simply for its physical function, such as the use in Figure 1.1, where a carrier bag is used to protect some tools, or simply for its appearance, as in Figure 1.2, where some bottles are displayed on a windowsill.

In most cases there is a mixture of influences on the decision to re-use something. Out of the various different types of packaging that are involved in what the British Standards Institution defines as 'the containment, protection, handling, delivery and presentation of products' (BS EN 13429:2000), it is what is known as 'primary' packaging that is most likely to be re-used in the home. This is the arrangement of materials designed to display, promote and contain the product the consumer takes home. 'Secondary' packaging is the pack that contains and transports primary packs and does not usually make it into people's homes. Another pair of terms is used to describe packaging re-use: 'closed-loop' and 'open-loop'. In closed-loop re-use, an item is used again for the same purpose as originally intended within a recognized distribution system – the classic example being the re-use of milk bottles in doorstep delivery. All other re-use is open-loop, where the pack is re-used in ways unforeseen by the designer and outside any externally managed system. It is this type of re-use that is the subject of this book – open-loop re-use of primary packaging that is defined only by the practices of everyday life.

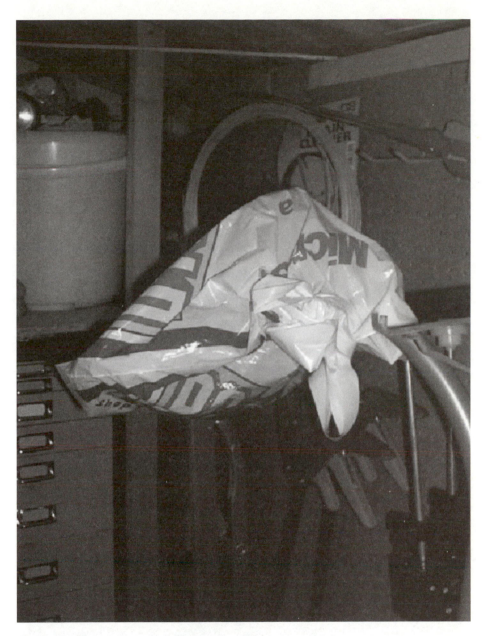

Figure 1.1 Carrier bag re-used to protect tools

Source: Authors

Figure 1.2 Blue glass bottles displayed

Source: Authors

Why Is It Important to Understand Packaging Re-use?

The simple answer to this question is that it is important because the open-loop re-use of primary packaging has been little studied and its potential benefit to environmental sustainability has therefore been unknown. The re-use that is the subject of this book has been largely ignored in debates about waste packaging, so although the debate has seen strong negative feelings expressed, calls to 'ban the plastic bag' for instance, how we actually deal with packaging in everyday life and the opportunities that exist to ameliorate the problem it poses through design have remained obscure. Although re-use features as one of the 'three Rs' of the packaging waste hierarchy – reduce, re-use, recycle – in the UK, industry, government, retailers and designers have tended only to consider closed-loop re-use. It would also be easy to get the impression that even this type of re-use has been considered marginal, judging by the emphasis on recycling and the low profile that re-use has in general.

There is heavy dependence on recycling as a response to packaging waste in the UK. Recycling requires a significant investment in fixed infrastructure for collection and processing and people's access to such facilities can lessen its effectiveness. In contrast, packaging re-use is a largely private activity which is not dependent on location and requires no civil infrastructure (Corral-Verdugo, 1996). Whereas it is very easy to demonstrate the effectiveness of recycling schemes, because it is possible to measure the tonnage of material recycled, by its nature this is not possible for open-loop re-use. The fact that its results are easily quantifiable makes recycling an attractive response to initiatives to lessen the environmental impact of waste, because these initiatives have often been driven by targets in tonnes of material recycled. This has led to other distortions in recycling efforts, for instance a concentration of efforts to recycle dense materials like glass at the expense of plastics.

A similar effect can be seen in efforts to lessen the tonnage of packaging produced in the first place. The UK's Waste Resource Action Programme (WRAP) has a programme to encourage impact reduction in glass packaging through its 'GlassRite' projects, which aim to save 60,000 tonnes of glass from entering the waste stream per year through reducing the weight of containers.[4] These projects focus on encouraging retailers, brand owners, packer-fillers and manufacturers to use and/or develop lighter glass containers in a number of market sectors. Again, they are politically attractive because they offer quantifiable reductions in waste.

While recycling and packaging reduction attract the attention of government because their benefits are easily quantifiable and serve established agendas for sustainable action, packaging attracts people's attention as a problem because of its visibility in the immediate environment. Our streets and roadsides glitter and twinkle with the lurid colours and eye-catching finishes of discarded packaging. While other issues of ecological sustainability, such as global warming, attract our concern but remain invisible to all but the trained eye of the scientist, the carrier bags that flutter in the winter breeze, caught in the branches of roadside trees or impaled on barbed-wire fences, upset our sense of how the environment should look. Global warming creates a diffuse worry, but waste packaging directly upsets our sense of order.

The convention in the UK for retailers to offer customers free carrier bags has made them a ubiquitous item that feels like a necessity; a part of the supermarket provisioning system that is responsible for increasing our dependence on all sorts of packaging. But calls to ban plastic bags demonstrate that our feelings about them are equivocal – they have become part of our everyday routines, but we object to the sight of them when they are misplaced. However, it has become clear over the last decade that these plastic carrier bags are routinely re-used, and the events that have brought this to light make a case

Figure 1.3 Plastic bag caught on a barbed-wire fence
Source: Authors

study, explored below, that introduces some of the key principles at work in other less visible instances of re-use.

Carrier Bags and Bin Liners – Current Concern about Packaging

According to the UK's Waste Resource Action Programme (WRAP), in 2006 UK consumers used about 10 billion plastic carrier bags – enough to reach to the moon twelve and a half times if laid end to end (WRAP, 2009).[5] Strenuous efforts by government and retailers have led to this figure being halved in the three years to May 2009, people's involvement in changing their habits being crucial to this reduction. The persistence of plastic carrier bags, their visibility in our surroundings as waste, as well as the fact that some end up in the marine environment has led to sufficient public concern that plastic carrier bags have drawn political attention and people have responded to efforts to reduce their consumption. Commenting in 2007 on retailers' efforts to limit the environmental impact of free carrier bags, Paul Bettison, Chair of the UK's Local Government Association Environment Board, identified consumers' habits as the culprit: 'Most people throw their bags straight into the bin once they've unpacked their shopping, which means the bag ends up being buried in landfill' (Bettison, 2007). But consumers have also been part of the solution.

While a proportion of the free carrier bags that UK consumers take home probably do go straight in the bin once they have carried shopping home, research that examines what consumer actually do with carrier bags in the home suggests something rather different is happening to this demonized packaging item, as well as to other types. The authors' research (Shipton, 2007), as well as the recent publicity about the consequences of limiting the supply of free bags, suggests that consumers in fact re-use plastic carrier bags in a number of ways. The factors that influence whether a carrier bag is re-used include the type of material it is made from, what it looks like and the brand it may represent. People report commonly re-using carrier bags as poop-a-scoop bags, sports kit bags, domestic bin liners, to carry other rubbish for recycling, for stopping up draughts in the house and, of course, when shopping. Such a list is limited only by the creativity of individuals and the ways that a carrier bag can fit in the pattern of their lives. In many of these applications, re-using the carrier bag precludes buying something else specially to do these jobs.

This re-use is largely invisible, but the bags that escape from the waste stream into the countryside are anything but. It may be this fact above others – that discarded plastic bags are often highly visible – that has contributed to pressure by environmental campaigners and the media to take positive actions that limit our consumption of plastic carrier bags. In 2002 the Government of the Republic of Ireland placed a levy of €0.15 on plastic carrier bags. As a result, there was a decrease in the number of bags distributed by retailers, with consumers instead carrying their shopping in bags designed to be re-usable or in paper bags (Irish EPA 2004, Irish Government Citizens' Information Resource 2009). According to environmental campaigners Planet Ark, the resulting 90 per cent reduction in the use of plastic carrier bags distributed at the till equated to over a billion fewer bags being distributed per year. However, because one of the most significant secondary uses of plastic carrier bags is as waste bin liners, one consequence of the levy was an increase in the demand for virgin plastic bin liners by around 70 million (Planet Ark, 2004 cited in Parliament of New South Wales 2005: 14). The policy was arguably a success in terms of reducing the ecological impact of shopping, though its benefits are debatable (Bickerstaffe, 2006), but more significantly in this context, the fact that the ban stimulated increased consumption of new bin liners demonstrates clearly that re-use makes an impact on consumption.

The continuing carrier bag saga also offers insights into the role of materials in packaging re-use more generally, particularly in relation to the relative willingness of consumers to re-use packaging made of different materials. In September 2006 Sainsbury's introduced their first re-usable carrier bag made from jute. As well as reducing the consumption of fossil fuels to make disposable plastic bags, a bag made from this material also seems more natural, less synthetic, because of the cultural associations that go along with it. Its beige colour, rough texture and slightly earthy smell add up to a powerful signifier of 'natural-ness'. The muted colours and soft textures of a jute bag make it appeal to shared beliefs about 'the goodness of nature'. The association of moral qualities with natural materials, particularly as they relate to ideas of nature, emerged along with the hippies in the 1970s and built on assumptions about the relative virtue of various materials that are found in the writings of William Morris and A. W. N. Pugin in the nineteenth century. According to these assumptions, wood, stone, cotton, linen and wool are good, authentic materials, whereas plastic is inauthentic and bad partly because it is 'unnatural' (Fisher, 2003). The carrier bag story suggests that people do re-use a proportion of the packaging that enters their homes. The following chapters of this book demonstrate that they do this for complex reasons – a network of factors influences re-use. But despite this complexity, it is possible to identify what these factors are and to relate them to one another. By doing so it should in principle be possible to design packaging with them in mind and therefore promote its re-use. Different types of people find different ways of re-using packaging by doing different inventive things with objects made of different materials. All of these activities give objects that would otherwise enter the waste stream another lease of life, in some cases deferring or replacing the purchase of another product to do the same job. But what sorts of objects are these bits of packaging that we process in our homes and may re-use? A look at the history of packaging can provide an answer.

An Extremely Brief Typology and History of Packaging

Many types of packaging are routinely re-used, and therefore it is appropriate to identify these different types and consider how they have come about. The following provides only a brief outline of the stages of the development of packaging; the topic is covered in much greater detail by others (Klimchuk and Krasovec, 2006; Soroka, 1996; Twede, 1998). Before industrially manufactured and packaged goods became common in the late 19th century, products were packaged by the shopkeeper using materials such as brown paper, waxed paper, tissue, cloth and string. These bespoke packages have been superseded by packaging that is designed to conveniently protect, promote and dispense products bought from self-service shops. It has recently become hard to work out what is product and what is package, particularly with toiletries, household products and cosmetics that only exist as saleable products by virtue of packaging that both carries them to us and makes it possible to use them.

The same range of technologies and techniques available to manufacture contemporary products is applied to packaging – from advanced materials such as nano-clays and bespoke plastic polymers to electronic circuits for radio frequency identification that can be printed onto a surface. Many packaging designs are visually sophisticated, such as spirit bottles, cosmetics packs and household goods incorporating distinctive shapes and clever dispensers. At the other end of the spectrum there are relatively low-tech, non-durable manufactured packaging designs such as corrugated board or cellophane wraps. This spectrum of low- and high-tech packaging reflects the spectrum of low- and high-tech products in manufacture and use.

Packaging has been needed for as long as people have had to store, move and preserve edible or fragile items. The earliest packaging was made by its user from whatever materials were available to create appropriate containers or protection for goods. When goods were traded, the need arose for different forms of packaging to protect and transport them. Packaged goods needed to be identified, and the first merchandise to carry printed designs is recorded in the mid 16th century (Kilmchuk and Krasovec, 2006). In the West, the onset of modernization from the 18th century – the expansion of cities, the development of technologies of production and transportation, the division of labour through mass production – was accompanied by new consumer products, transported in boxes, kegs, baskets and bottles. This increase in merchandise brought a need for packaging to protect and transport it and for branding to identify and differentiate one product from another.

While the new city-dwellers might not have had the space to buy in bulk, the shops where they bought their produce did. Goods were decanted into the customer's own containers or packaged in the shop in smaller portions for each customer. Until the mid 20th century, products were routinely packaged at point-of-sale using materials such as brown paper and string, and some still are – being served individually is a mark of distinction that is signified by an individually wrapped purchase from a delicatessen or up-market sweet shop.

While the hand-wrapped package has become reserved for luxury goods as a marker of their status, in the modern era, ready-made packaging began to function both as physical protection and to project symbolic content. Often the latter has centred on the identity of the product – its 'brand'. Brand names first appeared alongside modern consumption in the late 18th and early 19th centuries to allay suspicion among consumers of goods they no longer had any part in producing and at a time when many foodstuffs were frequently adulterated with poisonous substances (Coley, 2005). The brand itself evolved from being a mark used to identify the owner of an object (its origin coming from the hot iron used to identify livestock), to a mark which consumers could trust as a sign of purity and quality. With this, the function of packaging changed from offering only physical protection to being a communication and promotional tool (Baren, 1997; Soroka, 1996; Strasser, 1999).

Along with the development of the metal can in the 19th century, with its improved capacity to keep food fresh, came some of the characteristics of modern packaging that persist in the present. As well as being durable, it was possible to make metal packaging highly decorative and its durability ensured lasting impact for its visual design – branded packaging that would outlast its contents could continue to function as advertising. Manufacturers were able to give their brands enduring presence in consumers' lives through packs that were intended to be kept and re-used, as in Figure 1.4. Canning required the development and application of advanced technology and new materials, and manufacturing processes have continued to be developed to package different products, going hand-in-hand with symbolic impact. Other early mass-produced packaging – bottled beers, tins of snuff, bottled fruits, tins of mustard, tins of tobacco and tins of tea – used and extended material and processing technologies, also tying into advertising campaigns.

After the start of the 20th century, plastics began to be developed that were appropriate for packaging, such as cellulosic film in 1911, with Dupont's Cellophane being introduced in 1927 (Soroko, 1996, p8). Plastic packaging was attractive partly because the chemical origins of plastics – the sterility

Figure 1.4 OXO tin from the mid 20th century

Source: Authors

implied by their artificial origins – answered consumers' anxieties about the purity and safety of food and concern about contamination and infection from bacteria (Tomes, 1999). Plastic packaging not only could be marked with its manufacturer's identity, associating it with whatever qualities went along with their brand, but its materials in themselves connoted progressive modernity, as well as a distinct detachment from the messy reality of where food actually comes from. This latter potential in plastic packaging continues to be used routinely to make certain foods more acceptable – a piece of beef steak sealed in plastic film does not leak blood; food sealed in plastic is perhaps more obviously 'untouched by human hand' than its canned equivalent (Kubberod 2005, Fisher 2008b).

The packaging re-use discussed in later chapters includes a number of examples of plastic packaging being re-used, but people seem to operate with a hierarchy of materials that favours glass and metal at the expense of plastic, which may mean that the prospect of re-using it is less attractive. A durable metal package may be more likely to be considered re-usable because

17

its actual enduring qualities are accompanied by an association with strength and it is therefore not seen as a throwaway item. This association between materials and meanings was demonstrated in an exercise where people listed artefacts that they associated with wood, metal, plastic, paper/cardboard and glass. The responses showed that non-synthetic materials, even relatively ephemeral ones such as paper and cardboard, were mainly associated with products with a certain permanence, quality and display value, with metal being associated with cars, cookers, fridges, machinery and cutlery (Shipton, 2007, p89).

In the context of packaging, these associations have long been used by manufacturers to encourage the re-use of certain packs, with the effect of reinforcing their brand's presence in people's homes. From an early date, goods were packed in tins that were highly decorative, many being so good to look at that they were saved for other uses such as storing cakes, and intended to be by their designers. Some were designed with other secondary uses clearly in mind. For example, in the 1930s Crawfords biscuits were sold in a tin with a Lucy Atwell illustration that was designed to be used as a money box once the biscuits were finished. In this case the designers intended the tin to have a further use, as a money box, and also made it desirable as a work of art that carried the signature of the artist.

There are other examples of metal packaging from the early 20th century that were designed to be re-used. The OXO tin in Figure 1.4 has instructions printed on it that identify its intended secondary use as a sandwich tin. Some of these tins were, presumably, used to take their owners' lunch to work, but as they aged and became less acceptable for carrying food they took on other uses. In either application, they always carried with them their symbolic 'content' – promoting the OXO brand through its clear modernist graphic. This ability of packaging to serve a useful physical function as well as continuing to carry a strong message after the goods it contained were used up was put to use for patriotic purposes during World War I. At Christmas 1914 all members of the services were given a tin gift box out of a fund started by Princess Mary, the King's daughter. Once the tobacco and cigarettes they contained were used up, the tins were useful to keep valuable things dry in the trenches. At the same time, the symbolism of their embossed lids continued to carry its intended morale-boosting message.

These examples of packaging design encapsulate the basic elements of re-use that are discussed in the following chapters; however, despite the fact that it is easy to see in these examples the ways in which their designers intended the packaging to be re-used, and the commercial and patriotic messages it carried, it is not possible to know the uses these designs may have been put to apart from those envisaged by their designers. The designer of the OXO tin could not predict what would be stored in it, apart from sandwiches, or where, or for how long, or why. Neither could the designers of Princess Mary's tins know what uses members of the forces would find for their design – though there is anecdotal evidence that it was used to preserve items as diverse as bibles and letters from loved ones.

In summary, both the physical and symbolic attributes of packaging are relevant to its design, and both attributes are seen at work when it is re-used. The types of packaging that are re-used are those that are more durable and that survive their initial 'processing' in the home. They have two sets of characteristics that are in play as they are processed – they have certain physical properties (such as their materials) as well as symbolic attributes by virtue of their design, which may relate closely to their branding. So much for packaging objects. The other active agents in the processing of packaging in the home are the human beings who interact with packaging and the places in which they do so.

Domestic Spaces, Re-use Habits and Types of Consumer

This book aims to provide a greater understanding of how people re-use packaging in their homes, building on the idea of the home as a space where we process the things we bring into it. Gavin Lucas (2002) describes the home as a processing unit where packaging enters, is evaluated, categorized and then removed for disposal. Our actions are central to this process, as we decide the value or usefulness of each piece of packaging we encounter and what we should we do with it. We may not be conscious of many of these decisions, because they are part of the everyday ritual of sorting, classifying and disposing of items, and in the case of packaging, most often the result of this decision-making is to categorize it as waste and consign it to the bin, into the waste stream. Exactly how we do this, whether we sort it or take it to a recycling station, may be influenced by exhortations from the media and local authorities responsible for dealing with domestic waste.

This encouragement to recycle waste plays on ethical imperatives relating to the physical environment – we are encouraged to 'do our bit' for the environment by dealing with our waste appropriately. Given that we can achieve a sense of being an environmentally responsible citizen by simply conforming with the systems that waste management authorities provide for us, it is worth considering what might motivate people to divert packaging from the waste stream by re-using it. A decision to disrupt the 'natural' flow of packaging from front door to bin also requires action that is at least to some extent creative because it goes against the grain of the waste management systems that are provided for us. This creative element requires that we see a practical use or an aesthetic quality in a packaging object that did not feature in its original design; re-use makes a piece of packaging into a new object by ascribing to it a new use. While the creative moment that results in a particular person re-using a particular thing at a particular time in a particular place is likely to be influenced by the situation that person finds themselves in, some of the factors that motivate it may be shared. There may, for instance, be a stronger ethical 'feel-good' factor in re-use than in even the most responsible disposal of packaging for recycling and this may have a strong implication for the individual's self-identity. Re-used packaging may also simply perform a physical function that brings benefits to its owner (Defra, 2007b).

The common barrier to recycling – an individual's feelings that their efforts are insignificant as a 'power of one' – does not seem to inhibit re-use. Barriers to re-using packaging instead are as likely to be related to the physical arrangements of our homes and the embeddedness of our habits in dealing with packaging as waste. The time required to sort re-usable packaging from waste, the space that is available in the home to keep packaging that is waiting to be re-used, as well as the collection of cultural and social attributes that are summed up as 'lifestyle' may all constitute barriers to packaging re-use. It is tempting to link the range of these potential barriers to re-use to the absence of coordinated campaigns to promote it, reflected in the fact that when it occurs it emerges from the inventiveness and personalized everyday routines of individuals.

Because the spontaneous, inventive re-use of packaging that is the concern of this book has not received much attention from the perspective of environmental benefit, it is not clear how it relates to existing segmentation typologies for the population. For this reason, population segmentation in respect of pro-environmental behaviour may be of limited use to understanding how people re-use packaging and how to promote it through design. For instance, Defra's recent environmental behaviour segmentation model (Defra, 2008) divides the UK population into seven segments with distinct sets of attitudes and beliefs about the environment, which relate closely to issues like recycling or the frequency of flying, which are present in public discourse and which require more or less consciousness of the need for collective action. However, with the exception of concern about plastic carrier bags, much of the packaging re-use that takes place does not impinge on public discourse but instead is bound up with more private habits, inventiveness and creativity in response to immediate needs, thrift and other non-environmental factors.

Packaging re-use characteristically take place in domestic environments, so to understand it requires that we understand something of the ways that packaging flows through our domestic spaces.

Kitchens and Bathrooms:
The Engine Rooms of Packaging Re-use

Packaging materials and manufacturing have changed and developed along-side changes in household arrangements. Much of the contact we have with packaging takes place in our homes as we consume products, and in turn the design of homes and their influence on our patterns of life has a relationship to the ways that we may value and re-use packaging. The development of bathrooms and kitchens in response to drives for hygiene prompted by public health campaigns of the 19th century were particularly significant because this meant that products were designed specifically to be used in these spaces which themselves drew on developing ideas of cleanliness and disposability.

Gavin Lucas describes the history of domestic waste processing and the reorganization of the spaces of homes through the 19th century. It quite soon became standard practice to separate kitchen refuse from bodily waste, generating new standard items of material culture such as the indoor cistern toilet and the kitchen bin (Lucas, 2001, pp10–11). Lucas talks of kitchens and bathrooms as systems or 'economies' through which objects flow, with waste being that which is ejected from the system. From the late 19th century many of these ejected objects have been packaged commercial products, promoted through advertising. Some of the earliest of these were themselves cleaning products, which contributed to the demarcation of hygienic functions in the home, as well as to the flow of goods through it. For instance, in 1879 Proctor and Gamble started making its 'Ivory' soap, developing the brand as well as its associated packaging through print advertising.

Kitchens were also transformed by the increase in material goods. Lupton and Miller (1992) note that as well as being the place to prepare food, the kitchen has become the place where goods enter the home, and where waste packaging leaves it, along with most other sorts of waste. At the same time, modern kitchens have become mechanized, filled with permanent equip-ment that supports the range of functions relating to provisioning, cooking and sorting waste, that has served through its design to entrench modern attitudes to cleanliness and disposability (Forty, 1986). Packaging operates as one of the 'moving parts' of this permanent mechanical system. Along with water, electricity and food, packaging flows through our kitchens, brought in carrier bags, sorted and discarded in the waste.

But these domestic spaces do not have purely physical functions. Since they have become designed spaces they have accumulated a variety of asso-ciations – modern kitchens and bathrooms go along with with some powerful sets of ideas about how we should live. As Lupton and Miller and Forty explore in detail, their design has connected them with a concern that arose early in the twentieth century to achieve a version of industrial efficiency and clinical hygiene in the home, expressed through streamlined 'wipe-clean' surfaces. In parallel, in the later twentieth century, both types of space have often had over-lain on this industrially inspired approach a commodified version of vernacular style. Packaging interlocks with these environments not simply for its physical performance but also in the ways it is stylised to perform symbolic 'work' as part of these aestheticised domestic spaces. These spaces are continuously re-evaluated through fashion and a good deal of the symbolic work they do relates closely to the ways that people present themselves to others – the ways we arrange the details of our domestic spaces play a significant role in our self-presentation. The sociologist Erving Goffmann (1959) described how our physical surroundings provide settings for the performances that we stage as we create a persona that is appropriate for a particular situation. He identified three parts to the 'social front' that is constructed through the performance of self – 'setting, appearance and manner' (1959: 39). It is the setting of the social performances of everyday life that is relevant to the re-use of packaging, because when it is re-used it can form part of that setting.

Goffman's discussion of self-presentation concentrates on the perform-ance of human actors rather than the non-human ones that may comprise its setting. Nonetheless his dramaturgical metaphor for self-presentation provides a useful image through which to understand how packaging may be re-used in different ways in different parts of our homes. He talks of the 'front-stage' of a performance, where the intended impression is carefully managed through behaviour and 'decorum', in an appropriately arranged physical setting. This he compares to the 'back-region' or 'back-stage' that goes along with many performances. He uses the division between the kitchen and the dining room in a restaurant to illustrate the difference between back-stage and front-stage behaviour – a waiter's demeanour can change utterly between the two spaces. While the waiter may have been arguing heatedly with the chef before he leaves the kitchen, at the moment he or she passes through the kitchen door he will adopt the appropriate performance for the front-of-house role.

Goffman's focus on human actors in his discussion of the 'front-stage' and 'back-stage' of the performance of self can be adjusted to concentrate on the spaces that make up the 'settings' for self-presentation and the objects inside them. Doing this means extending somewhat from the possibility that Goffman identifies for objects and settings to be 'sign equipment' (1959, p46) – in other words to be made deliberately to function as symbols – to give them a degree of active power to stand in for people in their self-presentation, to allow people to project themselves through objects. It is possible, as Russell Belk (1988) does, to think of the objects that we surround ourselves with as extensions of our selves. This 'extended self' exists partly in the objects we control and surround ourselves with and it is stronger in them to the degree to which we can control them. Belk relates this principle to the desire to make collections of objects which are subjected to intense control, but James Carrier (1990) suggests that it is a property of all objects that we can call possessions.

When packaging is re-used it passes first through the kitchen, which is a space with a dual role – it can be both front-stage and back-stage. A desirable contemporary kitchen is potentially a space for gracious living and its design can be part of an 'extended self', and it is also where we undertake the physical processes of food preparation and waste sorting. Some of the packaging that gets sorted in the kitchen is re-used for a second life that takes advantage only of its physical attributes, whereas some serves a further purpose that draws on its symbolic properties. The former type of re-use often takes place in parts of the home that are relatively out of sight, relatively back-stage. In contrast, packaging sometimes makes its way to living spaces, selected for its symbolic content, carefully curated and displayed in these front-stage settings.

Ordering Systems and Types of Function: Fashion, Brands and Self-Presentation

Packaging requires sorting. Our main way of interacting with it is to order it, to categorize it, dividing it into what is useful and what is trash. It is our human regimes which govern this ordering; it is only partly defined by the material properties of the packaging object. In Susan Strasser's comprehensive account of the history of waste (1995), she notes that it is 'human behaviour [that] defines trash'. Mary Douglas (1966) argued more generally that not only our response to waste and disorder but what we define as waste and disorder depends on the patterns embedded in our culture.

The sort of patterns through which we classify objects that we want to separate ourselves from, to reject, have an equivalent, and opposite, in the patterns through which we find ourselves more or less attracted to things. To the extent that these patterns are shared, rather than personal, they are evident in configurations of taste and fashion. Taste and packaging re-use may not seem obviously related, since it is the physical function of packaging that is usually prominent in our efforts to manage its passage through our homes, but most packaging is also heavy with the symbolism that serves its function to carry branding. This aspect of packaging affects whether or not we buy a product – it is designed to promote sales – and it can also affect whether or not we are prepared to re-use leftover packaging. As we will see in the following chapters, the presence of branding can in some cases make it more likely and in others less likely that packaging is re-used.

Fashion and its relationship to our sense of self are among the strongest influences on the patterns of contemporary life. Many of the decisions we make about which things to buy, and which to avoid, are based on how they fit with our self-image, and often this is expressed as how fashionable we feel something is. This aspect of the re-use phenomenon can again be seen in the attention that carrier bags have attracted over the last decade. Early in this period, in October 2000, the potential of carrier bags to be practical, re-usable items as well as having symbolic functions that relate to fashion was demonstrated by the UK Government's Department for Environment and Transport claim that 'the humble supermarket carrier bag' was 'this year's favourite fashion accessory', being more popular to re-use than designer bags (DETR, 2000).

However, people are more prepared to re-use some supermarket carrier bags than others and consider them appropriate for some uses but not for others. People seem to order and classify carrier bags according to their physical properties, as one might expect – strong ones are more useful than weak ones – but the associations they carry are also very important. This ordering might relate to an association with the type of shopping that generated them – clothes shopping rather than everyday food shopping – or be to do with connotations of the brand they carry.[7] So the fact that a bag is from a fashionable shop might be one reason it is re-used; its strength might be another. Motivations to do with fashion depend on the characteristics of an individual, their age, gender, class and education, for instance. Consequently, symbolic content in a piece of packaging that promotes re-use by one person may prohibit it in another. The 'bag for life' that a middle-aged parent is proud to re-use may mean social death to their child if he has to use it to carry his sports kit to school.

Types of Function: 'Techno', 'Ideo' and 'Socio'

Another way of thinking about the different aspects of the re-use of carrier bags and other types of packaging is through ideas about different types of function. Archaeologist Michael Schiffer (1992) suggests that objects can have three different sorts of function. The most straightforward of these is 'techno-function' – whether the object is up to the job in hand. With packaging re-use this usually means whether the item is strong enough and the right shape to be re-used. The fact that fashion and self-image are important in re-use demonstrates that physical function is not the end of the story, however. The pride felt by the middle-aged parent re-using a carrier bag depends on a string of influences and social interactions that cause that person to have a conscience about the environment – its re-use is serving what Schiffer calls a 'socio-function' in signalling to others that the person has certain attitudes. Finally, and less frequently, there can be 'ideo-functions' that draw from sets of abstract ideas that we share. It may be possible to see such ideas evident in packaging re-use if it is motivated by thrift or a sense of duty to others.

Of course the function of an object is often designed into it – holding shopping is the 'proper' function of carrier bags. They are designed so they are strong enough for this techno-function and are printed with the right messages for an accompanying socio-function. Just as often, however, the function of a thing depends on where it is, who is using it and when. In this sense, function comes about because of the 'system' that an object exists in – it is defined by the object's context. Schiffer calls this 'system function'. By definition system functions cannot be designed into objects – they come about only in the process of people's interaction with them as they create systems for objects to function in. Sometimes objects can 'malfunction' in this sense. The adolescent boy who has to carry his sport kit to school in a 'bag for life' is carrying something designed to be proud of, but in the 'system' of a UK secondary school this function disappears – the bag loses its intended socio-function and becomes deeply uncool.

And it is not just children who have worries about such things that are intense enough to persuade them to re-use or stop them from re-using carrier bags. Figure 1.5 shows two designs of carrier bags for the European super-market chain Netto. The designs include the Netto logo and black Scottie dog symbol. It would be reasonable to assume that even though Netto is a cheap shop and its brand represents non-prestige, 'value' shopping, the striking black dog logo might encourage consumers to re-use the bag. However, Netto announced they had removed all the branding from their bags to encourage their re-use, having discovered that 'consumers prefer to re-use a bag if it is unbranded' (*Packaging News*, 2006). This suggests that, for some people at least, the connotations of the brand with economy, and perhaps poverty, are a disincentive to their re-using it.

Design strategies to promote re-use are more often positive than nega-tive. In 2006 the UK supermarket Sainsbury's recognized the potential for carrier bags to have a social function when they are re-used when they teamed up with Arts Council England to produce limited edition re-usable shopping bags designed by well-known artists Michael Craig-Martin, Anya Gallaccio and Paul Morrison. These 'art in your hand' bags were created to celebrate Arts Council England's 60th anniversary, promoting the environmental benefit of re-use as well as raising awareness of the impact of consumption on the environment and prompting debate about the role the arts play in people's lives. The Arts Council evidently considers art to be a powerful influence on everyday behaviour, suggesting that the bags would 'show how artists inter-vention can change the way people think and behave' (Arts Council England, 2006). Whether it is some ineffable power of art in itself that is likely to change people's behaviour with shopping bags or the social cachet of having some-thing to use every day that is endorsed by someone famous is debatable.

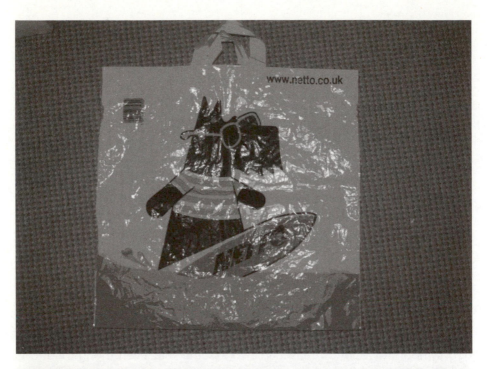

Figure 1.5 Netto carrier bags

Source: Authors

Alongside using high culture to promote carrier bag re-use, Sainsbury's other venture into re-usable carrier bags in the last decade was their well publicized and popular alliance with the UK accessories designer Anya Hindmarch. In early 2007 Hindmarch designed a limited edition re-usable shopping bag, made of canvas with a rope handle and carrying the slogan 'I'm NOT a plastic bag' in a quirky script (Sainsbury's, 2007). When it was released in April 2007, this bag, heavily trailed in the fashion press, sold out almost immediately. The unprecedented demand for such an everyday object was a function of the fashionableness of the object constituting a function in itself – it may not have had a strong connection to environmental concerns. While this is an extreme example, it demonstrates the relationship between the aesthetic aspect of packaging and its re-use that is evident in the more everyday examples that will be discussed in the following chapters.

Conclusion

In their discussion of the development of the design of kitchens and bath-rooms, Lupton and Miller emphasize that the standard for the 20th-century American kitchen did not come about as a consequence of modernist design, but was the result of an evolving practice that was deeply enmeshed with the development of modern consumption, involving what they call a 'commercial circle of consumers, journalists, manufacturers and advertisers' (1992, p48).[8] This circle identifies the actors responsible for the development of the normal conventions we follow when processing packaging – the conventions built into packaging itself which assume that it is ephemeral, to be used once only, and which draw on assumptions about cleanliness and convenience. The examples introduced in the following chapters show that even though this circle reinforces the idea that packaging is ephemeral – made to be wasted – some of it is re-used. The assumption behind this book is that only by understanding and following the ways these open-ended, unbidden re-use practices work, how they have grown up and what has influenced their development, is it possible to design packaging that works with them and promotes re-use.

The following three chapters take apart the phenomenon of re-use to think about it from three perspectives – in terms of the materials from which packaging is made, from the point of view of the make-up of the people who re-use it and by considering the spaces through which it circulates in the home. They draw from empirical work by the authors and discuss examples of packaging re-use, examples of the life of consumer packaging, in terms of these three points of view.

Notes

1   The *Cloaca Maxima* was the great sewer of ancient Rome and is still in existence.
2   The UK total for packaging waste produced in 2004 was 10 million tonnes, of which approximately 50 per cent was recycled or recovered (Defra, 2007a). There are projected to be 26 million households in the UK (Office of National Statistics), each of which therefore produced 0.38 tonnes of packaging waste. A medium-sized family car weighs approximately 1.3 tonnes.
3   There is significant scope for manufacturing new products out of recycled packaging materials without melting down the material, and companies are springing up that do this. One example is Doy Bags, a company based on a women's cooperative in the Philippines: see www.doybags.com.
4   See www.wrap.org.uk/retail/glassrite_projects.html.
5   Taking a carrier bag to be approximately 0.5m long, 10 billion of them would reach five million kilometres. The Moon is approximately four hundred thousand kilometres from the Earth.
6   Press and Cooper (2003, pp122–123) summarize Norman's discussion of 'user experience design'. He suggests that it requires experts with the following sets of skills to come together:

- Field studies specialists, with skills in anthropology and sociology;
- Behavioural designers, with backgrounds in cognitive science and experimental psychology;
- Model builders and rapid prototypers, rooted in computer programming, engineering and industrial design;
- User testers, who are skilled in rapid user-testing studies and may have a grounding in experimental psychology;
- Graphical and industrial designers 'who possess the design skills that combine science and a rich body of experience with art and intuition'; and
- Technical writers 'whose goal should be to show the technologists how to build things that do not require manuals'.

7   In the authors' research, a 43-year-old female interviewee described having different feelings towards different carrier bags, clearly distinguishing 'nice' bags associated with clothes shopping and carrying the brand of the store from other supermarket carrier bags:

> *Carrier bags – from IKEA I've got my little carrier bag storage thing – I shove them in that. If it's clothes shopping with posh carrier bags I put them in a different place. I'm quite sad with carrier bags – I keep the nice carrier bags.*

8   Lupton and Miller also note that the scientific management-influenced 'rational' schemes for kitchens still overlooked most of what actually goes on in them. Discussing Christine Frederick's early-20th-century schemes, they note that:

Numerous tasks have been omitted, such as putting away groceries, setting the table, consulting a cookbook, tending a child, stirring the sauce, wiping the counter-tops, adjusting the stove, discarding empty packages or preparing anything more complex than a single-dish meal. (1992, p46)

2

Material Factors

Introduction

The packaging that we encounter every day is made of a range of materials – paper, plastics, metal, ceramic, glass – and its design also involves some 'symbolic' content – text, shape, colour, pattern. As we saw in Chapter 1, both are important for the purposes that packaging is designed to fulfil and both are significant in re-use. Although it is convenient to consider these elements separately, and this chapter will emphasize the materials used in packaging rather than the symbolic consequences of packaging designs, this is an artificial distinction. Understanding packaging and its re-use in everyday life to promote its re-use through design means fully exploring the relationships between its physical and symbolic aspects – indeed, as we will shortly see, materials themselves have symbolic properties.

Thinking about the various materials that packaging is made from and their effect on the decisions people make to re-use it is a way of quite directly engaging with its 'materiality'. Whereas the distinction between 'material' and 'symbolic' is quite obvious – one relates to the physical stuff that objects are made of and the other to their cultural significance – the idea of 'materiality' is somewhat more subtle, though it has gained significant currency in the last decade or so. The recent popularity of the term in debates in a range of fields of study including sociology, anthropology, museum studies and archaeology relates to a move away from a tendency to think about people's relationships with objects as largely to do with cultural meaning, which emphasized their symbolic aspects. This tendency often employed theoretical approaches derived from linguistics, as if the life of objects could be understood fully by considering the relationships between them and people as a type of language. While this is often useful a useful way to think about objects, it is inadequate to the task of fully understanding our relationship to them.

Thinking from the perspective of design, this recent stress on materiality is welcome. There is a craft element to the best design training which means designers come to understand the properties of materials by using them. For all that an emphasis on the discursive elements of human–object relationships does make it possible to discuss their cultural significance in terms beyond the aesthetic boosterism that can characterize some design discourse, this discussion is incomplete if it cannot engage with the physical 'ground' of objects, their materiality. Recent debate in archaeology (Ingold, 2007; Tilley, 2007) demonstrates that this is not a novel realization in that field, even though debate about the appropriate way to engage with objects continues there. Talking of changes in the field of archaeology, Christopher Tilley notes that:

The discipline has now changed radically precisely because of a move from considering materials and their properties to considering materiality, or what these properties mean in different social and historical contexts and how they are experienced.

From the perspective of design, this means that to understand objects we need to honour our expertise with their materials, our craft-based knowledge of them, but in a way that embeds them in culture.

Materials affect us in everyday life. We respond to the world, are conditioned by it, partly because of what it is made of and what we have made it of. Tilley's concern as an archaeologist is to acknowledge that our sensuous immersion in a material world affects what we do, and what we think (p19). We are continually involved in exchanges with our material surroundings; they both facilitate our actions and constrain us. Sociologist Tim Dant (2005) calls these exchanges 'material interactions' with objects, proposing them as a kind of social interaction. These interactions may be grounded in an object's design – what it is made of and how it is constructed – and affected by properties that are not necessarily obvious, but are no less physical and 'material', such as form, weight, flexibility, texture, colour, resonance, smell and reflectivity. These are the properties that give materials their character, that give our exchanges with them their particular flavour. From the point of view of its re-use, the most significant aspect of the materiality of packaging is the degree to which its design and its materials make it open to modification. As we will see later in this book, designs that are open to modification may be more likely to be re-used than 'closed' ones, and this is a consequence of both their physical materials and their symbolic properties. If we re-use things we do so because we can, and because we can bear to.

Table 2.1 Tonnages of packaging materials going to landfill each year in the UK

Material	Tonnage in waste	Percent of total
Steel	175,000	3.5
Aluminium	134,000	2.8
Paper	931,000	18.5
Glass containers	2,500,000	50.0
Plastics	1,260,000	25.2
Total	5,000,000	100

A very straightforward way to understand the role materials play in packaging is to note their relative quantities in domestic waste. Recent work by Defra (2007a) has established that the main packaging materials appear in the UK domestic waste stream in the quantities given above each year.[1]

These figures indicate the tonnages of material that are truly 'wasted', in other words they are not recycled but go into landfill. It may be no surprise that plastics feature so prominently, given the relative difficulty of recycling these materials and their ubiquitous presence in every household bin, where the problem they constitute presents itself forcibly to us. We see plastic in our rubbish, as rubbish, more clearly than we see other materials. Their visibility as packaging waste, as a 'problem', may be partly responsible for the low value we consider plastics in general to have as materials. Even in applications where they are intended to be more durable, materials that can be identified as plastic may suffer from guilt by association with their use in packaging.

Material Connotations: Preferences and Properties

Materials are significant in themselves – in the abstract. We are used to this idea when thinking about precious materials such as silver, gold, precious stones and ivory. Grahame Clark (1986) has identified the historical meanings of such materials and the properties ascribed to them, including magical or curative powers. The authors' recent work (Fisher, 2004) suggests that everyday materials – the glass, metal, card and plastic that make up packaging – are no less significant, though the meanings associated with them are rather different. In the case of packaging, this significance affects people's preferences for packaging objects made of different materials, and therefore influences whether and how they re-use them.

An aspect of the significance of materials that is relevant to this discussion is the degree to which people think that different packaging materials have a negative impact on the environment. Research for the Association of European Board and Carton Manufacturers suggests that people think that cartons are the most environmentally friendly packaging materials, with glass a close second, followed by plastic then the metal in tin cans (Pro-carton, 2008). We need to take into account the fact that this research was commissioned by the carton board industry when weighing up this ranking of materials, but it indicates at least that it is possible to isolate the perceived sustainability of their materials as a factor in how people relate to packaging objects. This perception of environmental impact is likely to be influenced by the relatively strong presence of paper and card recycling in local government reclamation efforts and the consequent familiarity people have with the fact that paper

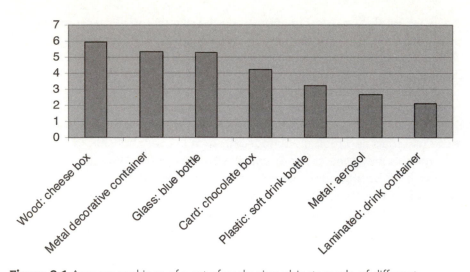

Figure 2.1 Average rankings of a set of packaging objects made of different materials

Source: Authors

and board can be recycled. The fact that it is possible quite easily to reclaim steel from general waste and recycle it into top-grade material is less likely to register in people's perceptions because it is depends on a process that is largely invisible. Also, the fact that paper and carton board derive from what is effectively a crop – they come from fibres that are grown – may also have a positive effect on people's perception of their environmental impact. Because of their vegetable origin they are 'natural' in a way that the other three materials are not.

Attitudes to materials are of course always combined with all the other factors that influence people's feelings about packaging, and asking people to rank objects of different materials demonstrates this. When interviewees were asked to put a set of seven packaging items made of different materials in order of preference, the average rankings were as shown in Figure 2.1. Although this exercise was carried out with only a small number of people as part of a qualitative interview, when the results are considered in terms of materials a hierarchy of preference is evident that runs from wood through glass to a combination of plastic and card laminated together. The fact that both the second and the sixth most preferred were metal packs demonstrates the significance of the other factors that are in play, the probable influence of the purpose that a piece of packaging serves and the effect of this on people's attitudes to it as an object.

It is safe to assume that the aerosol can is ranked near the bottom because

Figure 2.2 Lindt 'milk churn'

Source: Authors

of the object it is rather than what it is made of. Most people do not often encounter materials in themselves – they have always already been made into something and those 'somethings' bring along their own associations which affect what we think about them. Materials may influence preference between objects, and by extension our willingness to keep and re-use packaging, but they are only one factor alongside others. The decorative metal container in Figure 2.2 has been designed with a shape that is full of references to ideas about a good rural life, and this shared fantasy, which has no necessary connection to the material, may have been the element that makes it preferred over an aerosol of deodorant. However, the fact that the decorative container can be used for another purpose, can be re-used, whereas an aerosol can cannot, may also have influenced people's preference for it, and the durability of metal makes a second use possible.

The place where we encounter things also affects our thoughts and feelings about them, and the effect of this on packaging re-use will be explored in Chapter 4. The people who ranked the objects did so in their living rooms, which conventionally are places where decoration and appearance are as significant as physical function, if not more so. This may also have influenced the general preference for more decorative items over more functional ones in the ranking.

To a certain extent, though, the two rankings match up. In both it is a 'natural' material that is the most preferred, with glass preferred over plastic. This suggests that perception of the environmental impact of packaging materials may overlap with a general preference for them and that they bring along with them a certain weight of associations which are at work in the rankings. Each material has its own set of associations, its own character, which derives partly from the uses it is put to in our material culture, but which also has a strong relationship to its inherent physical properties; each has its own materiality. It is appropriate now to review the major packaging materials in turn from the point of view of the ideas that we find associated with them – each material has its own rich set of stories to tell.

Stories about Materials

Grahame Clark (1986) writes about the 'immaterial' properties that folklore has associated with precious materials. Other writers, such as Roland Barthes (1976) and Jean Baudrillard (1968), have treated materials as symptoms of contemporary culture. For Baudrillard, materials, wood for instance, contribute to the 'atmospheres' that contemporary interiors create. We do share assumptions about materials, including the apparently mundane ones that are used to make packaging. Each has a definite character, defined by the qualities which we assume it has. Each has certain connotations; certain meanings are associated with it. Given that these material characters clearly play a part in our relationships to objects, it is useful to review how they have come to be established, as well as what they are like now. This important material element of objects has acquired particular meanings, and these may influence packaging re-use.

Different classes of materials have been available for different lengths of time, and this seems to have a quite marked effect on their character. Natural materials[2] have been used for all sorts of purposes through human history and only lately for packaging, so they bring along to their application in packaging some of the connotations they have gathered through time from this variety of applications. Artificial plastics, by contrast, are a relatively recent invention and have been so heavily used for packaging that this use has itself been a significant influence on the character that we take them to have as materials. The following sections review four classes of materials: wood/paper, glass, metals and plastics. Although the emphasis in each case is on the symbolic character of the class of material, each also has a set of physical character-istics, and it might therefore seem inappropriate to dwell on their symbolic rather than their physical attributes.

But this emphasis is deliberate because, although the physical character-istics of materials are necessary for the function that they fulfil in packaging, there are two reasons why they are not the best place to start thinking about materials from the point of view of packaging re-use. The first reason is that packaging is re-used by people in everyday life because of what *they* under-stand of the objects they may or may not re-use. The physical characteristics of materials – their technical specifications – are often not obvious as we encounter them in everyday life, however important they are to designers and manufacturers. The second reason is that materials used in packaging are not honest characters. In fact they are habitual liars – materials that appear 'glassy' may be plastic; a metallic surface may be glass; polymers can be given the 'feel' of paper. These sorts of material deception mean that the symbolic and the physical properties of packaging materials do not necessarily coincide, and in many cases it may be primarily a material's symbolic properties that people recognize, rather than its physical ones.

Finally, this chapter will consider the ways that materials in combination may affect packaging re-use.

Wood and Paper: 'Natural' and 'Authentic'

Wood has a long history as a packaging material for storing and transporting goods in barrels, boxes and packing cases. For millennia before the industrial revolution, these applications went alongside its use to serve countless other domestic and industrial purposes. As a survivor from the pre-industrial era, wood carries along with it very well-embedded ideas that centre on conceptions of nature, even though it is not now often used in its raw form for packaging. In stark contrast, paper and card, which are wood-derivatives, are among the commonest packaging materials. It is quite easy to identify the connotations that accompany paper and wood by observing how they have been used in packaging, and these same connotations are evident in many of the ways these materials are used for other purposes. What we propose is that the connotations of paper and card when used in packaging quite often draw on the same symbolic vocabulary, the same connotations, as are associated with wood.

The visual character of wood is strongly evident when it is used to package speciality foods and high-status alcoholic drink, such as the Turkish delight box in Figure 2.3. The fibrous, directional structure that shows in its grain is always evident in the appearance of wood and this visual signature seems to be what connects it with the relationships that people have had with wooden objects in the past. This relationship originated early in human history, before

Figure 2.3 Turkish delight box

Source: Authors

the industrial era, since when wood has been processed quite radically to make industrial materials – plywood, chip-board, MDF. However despite its existence in these engineered forms, the character of wood has been defined to a lesser extent by its use in such technologically advanced forms than has the character of metals and plastics.[3] When it is used as a modern packaging material, therefore, wood brings with it connotations that contradict the associations that derive from the industrial origin of packaging itself. These 'woody' connotations are visible in, and reinforced by, its characteristic uneven, subtly modulated surface and its grain, and they are often employed by designers to give packaging a strong connotation of the natural and the hand-made.

The significance of this woody texture is so well embedded and well understood that it is easy to overlook its origins and how it works in detail. Pre-industrial life in northern Europe relied very heavily on wood. It provided houses, domestic objects – 'woodware', tools, shoes, furniture, ships, vehicles and machines. Indeed, the usefulness and availability of timber meant that it continued to be used in the machinery of the early industrial revolution, for instance in industrial textile production. The relationship between wooden objects and their forest origins is evident in the word used for archaic domestic small woodware – 'treen', which literally means 'of trees'.[4]

Since the early 1960s and the publication of Rachel Carson's *Silent Spring* (1963), anxiety about the ecological consequences of human activity, particularly the production and consumption of goods, has made the connotations of wood relevant in a new way. Its strong presence in pre-industrial human history and the fact that it is renewable because it grows out of the ground and can be re-planted combine to give it very powerful positive ecological associations. These associations are easy to invoke when wood is used in packaging, or other design, because of the way its inconsistent textured appearance marks it out visually. In everyday usage these associations are often summed up by the word 'natural', and in contemporary discourse that which is natural is often taken to be good. On close inspection, though, the powerfully positive ideas that go along with the word are very complex. Along with the sense of what is natural being the opposite of what is man-made go ideas about nature being the source of an authentic reality – this is the sense indicated in 'human nature' or when the word is used to indicate a person's innate character; their 'nature'.[5] This sense of authenticity and moral worth is very often played out in what we think about natural objects, particularly our surroundings such as woodlands and farmland. These ideas about the natural feature in discussions of how we relate to the environments we think of as natural, for instance Phil McNachten and John Urry's (2000) discussion of the contemporary consumption of woodland, which suggests that ideas of nature define spaces that are a contrast to industrial modernity and play out in our relationship to woods as what they call the 'natural other' to the modern.

Traces of these ideas accompany any object that has 'woody' qualities, even when it is not made of wood. Such objects might simply be printed with the grain of wood – that is enough to invoke the connotations indicated above and is a strategy that packaging and other sorts of design often adopts. As well as its visible grain, the fibrous structure of wood also gives it a characteristic texture to the touch, which is similar to the textures found in paper and card. Although they have a shorter history as materials encountered in everyday life in Europe,[6] and rely on industrial processes in their production, these very common packaging materials can also sustain some of the same connotations that come along with wood. Paper and card also happen very often to be physically and economically appropriate for packaging applications, but in this discussion it is their connotations that are of interest. While the texture of paper and card does not derive from a directional structure – they do not have a grain like wood – they share some of its tactile qualities and when unbleached have a 'woody' colour and tone. The effect of this last quality, and its relationship to the ethics of nature outlined above, is demonstrated by a research participant who told of sorting and saving paper bags for her husband to use for seeds. She would save brown ones, but discard white ones as inappropriate. There is no difference, presumably, between the performance of the two colours of paper in keeping seeds fresh, but in this application, for this individual, the colour makes a difference. It seems that the 'fit' between the woody connotations of brown paper and the pattern of associations that comes along with the activity of gardening, which itself includes ideas about nature, determines this choice to re-use one type of bag but not the other.

Glass and Ceramics:
Hygienic, Mouldable and Crystalline

The development of industrial techniques for the production of glass containers broadly coincided with the history of packaging, though people have been making and using glass for 6000 years (Macfarlane and Martin, 2004).[7] It was the production of glass vessels in standard sizes, in large quantities and for low cost that made them appropriate for packaged goods that required standard sizes and shapes and using forms and details that could communicate the brand identity of the products they contained. Joseph Owens's 1903 patent for machinery to mass produce blow-moulded bottles, along with refinements to the process in the 1920s, brought this technology to a point beyond which it has not since progressed. While wood, and consequently paper and card, have a ready association with nature that speaks through their colour and texture, the very different objective properties of glass and ceramics are more neutral, but perhaps bring with them connotations of artifice, played out across the sealed surfaces of objects that we take to be impermeable and know to be fragile. Glass has a mysterious character. Although it is made of simple ingredients, this belies the art required to manufacture objects from it. It attracts us because of its special qualities and because it shares properties with other materials. It can shine like polished metal; it can sparkle like precious stones; its colours can glow like the richest textiles; it can be made to take any shape.

Like wood and paper, glass has positive connotations in itself, though they are quite different in kind. As just suggested, some of these derive from its objective qualities and some from its similarity to other materials that are rare or valuable. Together, these give glass connotations of opulence, riches and high quality which are often drawn on in packaging designs, such as the perfume bottle in Figure 2.4. These qualities give glass objects in people's homes, including re-used glass packaging, the potential to signal their owner's taste and discernment. This means that the attractive qualities of glass packaging and its ability to chime with prevailing taste can influence its re-use in the 'front-stage' region of people's homes. For example, the glass bottle in Figure 1.2 has been re-used for decoration; a 'socio-function' has been found for it as part of an ensemble of objects in a domestic interior. The properties of its material have been emphasized by removing the label, which draws attention to the shape of the bottle, and by its position on a window-ledge, where daylight maximizes the effect of the deep colour and reflective surface.

Glass has other connotations, which also relate closely to its physical qualities and which affect its use and re-use for what seem more like 'techno-functions'. The fused and impermeable surface of glass has a positive effect on people's willingness to use glass containers for containing food and drink. Although this relationship between the fused surface of glass and our willingness to drink out of it seems a straightforward matter of physical function, it has some quite complex, deep-seated and sometimes metaphysical aspects, because it involves our bodies. Discussing beliefs about contagion, Rozin and Nemeroff (1990, p210) note that in Hindu custom containers with permeable surfaces such as wood or earthenware are considered more likely to convey spiritual pollution because of what their surfaces are like, even though this type of pollution is 'immaterial' and therefore can have no physical relationship to the qualities of the material. It is possible to rationalize this concern by relating it to the possibility of contamination by microbes that might lodge in a porous surface, but the practice of avoiding porous containers for food predates the discovery of bacteria in the 19th century and so the belief in the contaminating properties of porous materials does not require this knowledge. This suggests that it is the hard, shiny, impermeable qualities of a glassy surface themselves that make people feel confident that glass will preserve

Figure 2.4 Glass perfume bottle

Source: Authors

the purity of foods – purity against contamination by dirt of any sort, whether material or immaterial, whether defined by patterns of belief validated by science or by religion.

'Closed-loop' systems of packaging re-use have frequently employed glass containers. From the late 19th century, closed-loop systems grew up for bottles used for various sorts of drinks – beer, milk and lemonade being perhaps the best known. While the physical durability of glass made these systems possible, because glass containers will stand up to the vigorous sterilization process necessary to make closed-loop re-use work, it may be that the tendency to trust glass containers to be safe that derives from the quality of their surface affected the willingness to accept this type of re-use system. Although in the UK these systems have become less common than they were – milk bottles and one brand of lemonade are the only closed-loop re-use systems that persist – glass is still considered a 'premium' packaging material and is employed by designers because it is seen to have value in itself. This value derives from both its visual qualities – it is attractive – and the trust in its safety that derives from them.

However, despite the clear influence of the physical properties of glass on the way it works for us, it would be a mistake to assume that the connotations of glass are fixed by its material properties. The complex social exchanges of which objects are part mean that a particular physical attribute – form, colour, texture and so on – can acquire meanings that have no necessary relationship to it – as words do in a language. A story about the colour of glass bottles and the minutiae of prejudice in the 19th-century British Army illustrates this point. The 'case of the black bottle' became a cause célèbre in 1840. Lord Cardigan, the commanding officer of the 11th Light Dragoons, was outraged by the sight of a black bottle on the table at a formal dinner in the officer's mess, assuming it contained 'porter' – a drink associated with the labouring class. His fury was directed at one of a group of officers who had served in India, where they had commonly drunk bottled porter. Lord Cardigan took the opportunity provided by the appearance of the black bottle to systematically humiliate the officer in question, because he considered these 'Indian' officers lowered the social tone of the regiment. The bottle actually contained Moselle wine, but this fact did not counterbalance the opportunity that the negative connotations of its material provided Cardigan to emphasize his social superiority. In this rather special context the bottle acquired an unfortunate 'socio-function' (Hastings, 1986, p253).

These two stories show rather well the two ways in which materials influence the materiality of our interactions with objects. The Hindu prohibition against porous food containers points to the significance of the fixed physical properties of materials; the black bottle incident shows the fluidity of the play of meanings over the material reality of objects that draws from, and feeds, the social interactions of which they are part. These two aspects of how materials work for us, the physical and the social, are also evident in the next class of 'stuff' we will consider in relation to packaging – metals.

Metal: Strength, Durability and a Decorative Surface

The widespread use of metal for packaging directly coincides with modern industrialization. Before the modern era, metal utensils were common in people's homes – cutlery of iron or silver and copper cooking utensils, for instance, as well as brass used for clocks and watches and lead for roofs and windows. Less common as possessions, but still likely to influence people's understanding of what metals could do, were the decorative objects that took advantage of the gleam and colour of polished metal, whether the 'gold' of polished brass or the sparkle of precious metal in jewellery and church plate. Metals used in the domestic environment therefore combine two sets of qualities: they are strong and useful for physical tasks and their surfaces give them the potential for luxurious decoration. Making packaging out of metal has quite complex consequences for its re-use, which depends on both the potential for an object to physically stand another use as well as its acceptability; both techno- and socio-function are in play and relate to each other. Like wood/paper and glass, metals have strong positive connotations: they are at the same time durable and decorative. However, there are two sides to the 'identity' of metals as a packaging material, which derive from the particular uses to which they have been put. While their visual properties can create packaging with high-value connotations that is prized enough to be commonly re-used, such as decorative tins, the widespread use of canning to preserve relatively cheap food has given metal packaging a low-status identity too.

The most significant form of metal for modern packaging has been 'tinned' steel – steel coated with a thin layer of tin to stop it rusting and made into cans for food and containers for many other types of product. Its widespread use in packaging required the development of thin tinned plates of iron, and later steel, the production of which material was itself a significant industry (Minchinton, 1957). The canning of food originated with Napoleon's desire in the first years of the 19th century to solve the problem of provisioning his armies. A Paris confectioner, Nicolas Appert, responded to a government competition to develop a means of preserving food with a process for sealing it in glass jars and then cooking the whole thing, jar and all. Tin-plated iron was soon used as a more durable alternative to glass for this 'canning' process. Appert published his work in 1811, and once mechanized processes were perfected, canned food reduced in price and became popular. It was adopted enthusiastically by governments to feed their armies and by explorers in the 19th and 20th centuries. The lasting qualities of this metal packaging are demonstrated by the preservation in good condition of supplies from Captain Scott's ill-fated 1910 polar expedition at the hut at McMurdo Sound in the Antarctic.[8]

At the same time as it became popular and widely consumed during the early 20th century, tinned food gathered negative connotations among the cultural elite. Precisely because it was by this time cheap and plentiful, intellectuals and artists came to associate it, and by extension the people who ate it, with a lack of authenticity and a disconnection from both nature and respectable culture. For writers from T. S. Eliot to John Betjeman, tinned food came to signify the 'massification' of culture and to be associated with poor nutrition (Carey, 1992, pp21–22). This impression persists – although canning requires no preservatives to be added to the food and treats it only by heating it, the idea persists that tinned food is adulterated in some way and significantly less nutritious than fresh food. What such arbiters of taste thought about other sorts of steel packaging than tinned food is not clear, but there were plenty of examples of it from the mid 19th century. Many of these lent themselves to re-use and some were designed with re-use in mind.

The ability to print promotional messages on metal packaging and to emboss box-lids to reinforce and enhance printed images and patterns was exploited to produce items that would endure because of their material, would be attractive enough that they would be kept for a further purpose and would continue to advertise their original contents. Examples of decorative biscuit tins from the early 20th century are still plentiful and desirable and their continuing popularity is suggested by the contemporary tin in Figure 2.5, which is printed and embossed with a design made up entirely of images of past decorative biscuit tins made for McVities. These tins were produced by a number of firms, including Barringer Wallis and Manners of Nottinghamshire, and were used to package many other goods as well as biscuits. Barringer Wallis and Manners were bought in 1895 by John Player and Sons, the tobacco manufacturer, to provide tin boxes to package the cigarettes that were rapidly gaining popularity.[9] The range of applications for tin-plate packaging at this time is indicated by the fact that as well as litho-printed boxes for biscuits and cigarettes, Barringer Wallis and Manners also made confectionary boxes for Rowntrees of York.

The mid-20th-century OXO tin in Figure 1.4 was made to hold stock cubes. Its design carries a litho printed message emphasizing the potential to re-use this sturdy tin: 'this tin makes an ideal lunch box'. It seems likely that this 'designed-in' re-use was assumed to depend on the tin's physical properties – it was taken to be a functional rather than aesthetic matter, the tin was

Figure 2.5 Decorative tin; images of tins

Source: Authors

'ideal' because of its shape and size and its close fitting lid. But like the biscuit tin in Figure 2.3, its design also had symbolic aspects, which since the later 20th century and into the present has meant that tins like this have become attractive curios, their revaluation playing on nostalgia for an earlier phase of modernity. Recent metal packaging designs continue to take advantage of this dual capacity of the material – to offer both sturdiness and durability beyond the lifetime of its function as packaging and opportunities to play with the symbolic content of the pack. The design of the container in Figure 2.2, for instance, is a variation on a chocolate box, which is a type of packaging that people routinely value enough to keep and re-use. Here, the steel of the package has been coloured gold and given different textures in different parts. The material qualities that contemporary manufacturing processes make possible give this steel container a set of characteristics that mean it is neither simply a surface that can be decorated or printed on, nor an obviously 'steely' object. The form, colour and textures of this object are not characteristic of the material itself; rather they are representations of other materials and another object.

This is a playful object, which makes only a sidelong claim to authenticity – it is golden, but it is not gold; it is shaped like a milk churn but it is clearly not one. There is little about it that relates to conventional packaging for chocolate except that it uses colour to bring the connotations of luxury and beauty that accompany all things golden. The form it has been given is clearly what was intended to carry the marketing message for its contents, emphasizing the amount of milk in the chocolate it contains. The industrialization of milk production has passed beyond the use of milk churns, so its shape is to an extent nostalgic, detached from contemporary reality and located in a consumption fantasy about 'good chocolate'. It was one of the most preferred packs in the ranking test discussed earlier, perhaps partly because its initial contents were delectable. Although its contents may play a part in making it attractive, its curiously dissembling design did not diminish this, which suggests that although materials that have a strong sense of authenticity are valued, such as wood and paper, this is not a necessary feature in a pack that people feel positively enough about to re-use.

Surface effects are often now independent of the materials that carry them, and this dissociation between what one might think of as the 'inherent' qualities of a material on the one hand and its appearance on the other is a common feature of much contemporary packaging. A steel container can appear to be brass (or gold), glass can appear to be silvery steel, what appears to be paper or wood can turn out to be plastic. It seems that almost any material can take on the appearance of almost any other material, and because packaging designers are ever striving to find eye-catching, but cheap, finishes that will carry the appropriate semantic payload to make products appeal to a heavily segmented market where taste and style distinction is all, if an effect can be achieved, then some designer somewhere will have found a reason to use it. It is the plastics that can achieve this sort of subterfuge most effectively, and it is to these prime packaging materials of our age that we now turn.

Plastics: From the Quintessentially Modern to the Great Chemical Pretender

The history of plastics is relatively short, but this family of materials has seen rapid and intense development since the first artificial cellulose plastics were developed in the mid 19th century.[10] The century and a half since has seen these materials develop from relatively unreliable formulations quite closely related to the natural plastics – horn, shellac and rubber – and restricted in their application by their distinct physical limitations, to the family of materials we know today, which have physical properties that are built into them by their chemical specification and through production processes to achieve a bewildering variety of aesthetic qualities and physical capabilities. The 1.2 million tonnes of waste plastics that arise from packaging each year in the UK confirms its ubiquity as a packaging material – if such a confirmation were needed. From our everyday experience of regular trips to the supermarket, we know the significant quantities of packaging waste we generate and that much of it is plastic. Because of its prevalence as a packaging material, plastic has a significant presence in packaging re-use, and the qualities that we perceive it to have are therefore significant in working out how to encourage re-use through design.

In its history plastic has had both positive and negative connotations – often both at the same time in different applications. The earliest celluloid plastics were developed by Charles Wesley Hyatt in the 1860s to substitute for the scarce and expensive ivory needed up to then to make billiard balls. An association between plastic and imitation persisted. As well as making a good imitation ivory, celluloid was used to imitate starched linen for men's detachable shirt collars and vulcanized 'hard' rubber which could pass for ebony was known as 'ebonite'. This connection with imitation was cemented by the names that some new formulations were given, such as 'Ivorine'. This imitative potential persists in the use of plastic to produce the striking effects which are often deployed in packaging – the 'metallic' surface of a pack for a premium product, the container that appears to be wood, the 'paper-like' pack for cheese, the 'glassy' clarity of a container for bottled water.

This aptitude for pretence, this ability to dissemble, has consequences for people's feelings about materials, because these effects are so clearly not authentic – they have nothing of the 'truth to materials' ethic that became so strongly embedded in Western culture as a result of the work of William Morris and John Ruskin and the Arts and Crafts Movement at the end of the 19th century. To the extent that objects reflect people, materials that are considered inauthentic can be taken to imply inauthentic people. This was certainly the case for the 19th century clerk who could afford celluloid collars but not starched linen ones, and therefore, because the celluloid collar was good imitation, hoped to pass as more genteel than his income warranted. While contemporary culture very often has a more ironic and playful approach to the issue of authenticity – there are still rules, but more flexible ones – the relationship between plastic and an undesirable social fakery persists.

In parallel to this heritage of imitation, the novelty of plastics means they have been identified very strongly with modern progress. This progressive connotation has a basis in the genuinely startling properties of some plastics, the materiality of formulations such as cellophane, invented in 1908. The ephemeral, sparkling clarity of this material inspired its use in theatre costumes and stage sets that celebrated modernity (Brown, 2008). The surrealist artist Man Ray photographed a model in a cellophane dress in 1930, concentrating on the light-reflecting properties of the material (International Centre of Photography, 1990). A number of publications around the time of the Second World War, which had stimulated the development of some now familiar polymers such as the clear acrylic sheet used for curved windows in aircraft, promised that such new materials would help to bring about a seamless, clean, hygienic and stylish new world after the war (Plastes, 1941; Yarsley and Couzens, 1942; Gloag, 1945).

These days, however, when we notice plastic materials in everyday life, they are as likely to be characterized by negative associations as progressive ones, particularly when they have been employed in packaging and so constitute a visible waste problem that brings along with it feelings of disgust or of guilt in people so disposed. While these negative connotations do not seem to stop us consuming it, once plastic packaging has done its job, it is associated with waste and environmental degradation through litter. As noted in Chapter 1, the flimsy plastic carrier bag still conventionally given free at supermarkets has been the focus of campaigns that seem to make it a scapegoat for the wider environmental impact of our consumption of goods.[11]

It is the persistence of plastic in the environment, the visible ugliness of plastic film caught on fences and flapping in hedges, as in Figure 1.3, combined with the assumption that plastics are disposable, that seems to be a ready stimulus for people's negative views of the material. However, this association with ephemerality, this assumption that plastic goods are transient and should be treated as disposable, has not always applied to packaging, and therefore, in principle, it is possible to move our attitudes and opinions about the material away from it in the future. Jeffrey Meikle notes that in America before the Second World War, some packaging for expensive goods used 'beetle', an early thermosetting formaldehyde resin the formulation of which allowed brightly coloured items to be produced. Meikle suggests that these resins were accepted by the public in the 1930s partly because of their durability and high physical performance, and that this made them appropriate and acceptable for premium packaging in applications where glass might previously have been used.

The new polymers that entered people's homes in the post-war period initially drew on this association of plastics with durability that had been developed before the war – the polyethylene used in 'Tupperware' was both soft and durable; it had what Meikle calls 'resistant flexibility'. However, this perception was to change, not only through consumers' interactions with these new materials, but also because of market and industry pressures that derived from the oversupply of polythene. When polythene, which on its introduction was more expensive than glass, became cheap and over-plentiful, assumptions about its design, production and consumption also changed. Meikle quotes an industry commentator in 1956 suggesting that disposability was 'an important key to continuing volume' and that plastic's future was 'in the garbage can' (Meikle, 1995, pp77–78).

Assumptions about the disposability of plastics that derive from the economics of its production are likely to have a marked effect on people's willingness to re-use plastic packaging. But plastic materials also have inherent characteristics that may make us disinclined to use plastic packs again, especially around food. Whereas we know the surface of glass objects to be 'fused' and utterly impermeable, experience shows us that this is not so for plastic objects. Contemporary consumers report that plastic containers used for highly coloured food take on the colour of the food (Fisher, 2004). Because they are also aware of the chemical origin of plastics, this raises significant concern for them about how palatable food may be if it is stored in plastic containers. This staining graphically demonstrates that plastic is not fused like glass, but permeable. It implies that if food can stain plastic, then the chemical nature of plastic may taint food. This worry is not a recent phenomenon. The archive of the DuPont Company contains market research material from the 1970s that identifies consumers' misgivings about plastics, including reports relating to work done by a packaging designer, Irv Koons.

Working for a competitor of Tupperware in 1974, Koons discovered a significant dislike of the way that plastic containers become stained. His report noted that:

> Most of the women feel that Tupperware is expensive and very functional, but it does take on stains too easily, especially from sauces and gravies. They find that they can't remove the stains, and this is a serious negative. They try a variety of techniques to clean these products; however, none of them seem to work satisfactorily.[12]

Koons was working on a design proposition to seal the surface of plastic containers with an airtight coating. This, however, drew a strongly negative reaction from his participants that he summed up in this way:

> The idea of a new process for 'coating' a container immediately raised either negatives or questions. They were very concerned about the nature of the coating used. In light of many current revelations regarding dangerous chemical substances presently in use ... consumers are very hesitant about accepting any new, as yet untested, chemical agents in their home environment.

This sort of worry reflects the ecological concern that had grown up since Rachel Carson's work in the early 1960s and its marked influence on people's feelings about the effect of environmental pollution on their health. These feelings are still evident today; indeed people may now associate the ecological consequences of contemporary life with consequences for their own health more strongly than they did in the 1970s, given the succession of 'food scares' in the last 20 years or so. Koons suggested that this disquiet at the health effects of everyday chemicals, including those that make up plastics, was especially strong in 'women who are involved in health foods', suggesting that different segments of the population were likely to behave differently in response to 'scares' about the health effects of materials. This continues to be the case, since attitudes to health and the environment are not consistent through the population. People's attitudes and beliefs about the environment in general are not consistent either, and the extent to which this influences packaging re-use will be the subject of the next chapter.

The influence of ideas about plastics on people's willingness to re-use plastic packaging is clearly relevant to packaging re-use, given the prevalence of plastic as a packaging material. The physical properties of much plastic packaging – its built-in disposability – mean it can serve no further purpose after its contents have been unwrapped and it is destined for disposal. However, a proportion of the plastic packaging that enters the home has physical properties that mean it does offer the potential for re-use. This may be dependent on the material in itself – it may be rigid enough or it may be possible to clean it effectively enough for it to meet a further purpose – or the format into which it has been designed may mean that it affords re-use. In either case, however, the connotations of the material a pack is made of are likely to affect an individual's willingness to re-use it.

Artificial and Natural Materials in Combination, with People, in Culture

Many examples of contemporary packaging design employ materials in combination; this ranges from simple paper labels glued to containers to complex laminates of different materials – plastic and aluminium, for instance. While the combination of materials in packaging poses challenges for recycling because it is often not easy to separate them out economically, it is the much simpler combinations of containers and labels that are likely to be problematic for domestic re-use. The sophisticated combinations of materials in packaging films, for instance, are usually not evident as we interact with packaging in everyday life, but the authors' research has shown that when it is impossible to remove graphics and printing from packs, they may be less likely to be re-used. People seem to like to be able to bring containers to a state of tidy neutrality, free of graphics and labels, before they consider them suitable to re-use.

The packaging for pesto shown in Figure 2.6 plays on this desire to 'tidy up' some types of packaging to make them suitable for re-use, which will

Figure 2.6 Pesto packaging

Source: Authors

be further explored in subsequent chapters. This desire points to the ways in which, through their processing in the home, packaging objects are integrated into their owner's domestic arrangements. Their identity is changed and they are retrieved from the collective symbol world of consumption; they are domesticated (Silverstone and Hirsch, 1992). The role that their materials play in this process is significant. Packaging made of different materials is integrated into the domestic environment through use in different ways – the different materials lend themselves to different ways of being re-used, in combination with the other factors that influence the decision to re-use, or to store, or to dispose of an item.

The decision-making involved in each instance of re-use combines ideas about materials with the way the person making the decision thinks about the process, their habits, the social mores that influence them, as well as the physical demands of a function that a piece of re-used packaging might perform. The examples considered later in this book explore some of this complexity and the next chapter considers particularly the influence of those ways of thinking and social mores, but it is clear that materials play a significant part in re-use decisions. However, assumptions about which materials are more environmentally 'good', for use in packaging or other applications, may be confounded by these examples of re-use precisely because of the complex relationship between the packaging object, the individual who re-uses it and the domestic spaces in which this re-use takes place.

So making packaging of paper or carton board, which on the face of it may seem to be 'good' materials from an environmental point of view, may or may not facilitate its re-use, because of the materials' lack of physical durability, or because the connotations that accompany it are inappropriate, or because it cannot be made sufficiently neutral to fit into a particular domestic scheme. On the other hand, in the right context, making packaging out of card or paper may facilitate its re-use – the connotations of authenticity that accompany paper and card may make it particularly acceptable for a further use by marking it in a positive way. The aesthetic connection with an object, the positive feelings that enable an extended relationship with it, may be aided by the materials especially if they serve to enhance the sense of 'extended self' introduced in Chapter 1.

Certainly, the cultural power of materials has not been lost on significant commentators. Roland Barthes and Jean Baudrillard both made strong claims about the significance of different materials that are relevant to packaging design. In two exquisitely written and highly observant short articles, Barthes discusses the meaning of plastics and of toys (1976, pp53–56 and 97–100). This approach is framed by Barthes's discussion of the ideological function of myth in contemporary culture, in which he adopts semiology as his tool. The discussion in this chapter of the connotations of materials is indebted to these two articles, written between 1954 and 1956. They were based on his desire to 'reflect … on French daily life' and to 'analyse semiologically' the 'language of mass culture' (pp11 and 9), and both make much of the dubious relationship of plastics to ideas of nature.

Barthes writes in an entirely negative way about plastics in the toys article, introducing his discussion with a commentary on the 'usefulness' of many toys – their status as instruments for the socialization of children. He compares these with more abstract toys that offer opportunities for children's creativity and goes on to associate the qualities of both types of toys with his perception of the characteristics of their materials. He suggests that 'current toys', which he has characterized as overly functional, 'are made of a graceless material, the product of chemistry not of nature. … Moulded from complicated mixtures, the plastic material of which they are made has an appearance at once gross and hygienic; it destroys all the pleasure, the sweetness, the humanity of touch.' (p54)

In contrast, he describes wood positively in terms of its softness, quietness and 'natural warmth' and finishes the article with observations on the different manner in which the two materials 'die'. Wood fades in a humane way, whereas plastic is implicated in the death of toys that 'disappear behind the hernia of a broken spring' (p55). He invokes an idealized pre-modern oneness with nature where 'wood makes essential objects, objects for all time'. The article implies that this material essence is transferred to the children through playing with a wooden toy, as if they thereby could find their own true inner nature, their own essence.

Jean Baudrillard's discussion of plastics in a section of his *System of Objects* titled 'Natural Wood/Cultural Wood' also investigates ideas of the 'natural' and 'unnatural' (1968, pp37ff). But unlike Barthes, who holds to 'nature' as a real and unproblematic category, Baudrillard suggests that we must question whether 'natural' materials, like wood which 'lives and breathes and labours', still have any meaning *because* of the existence of plastic substitutes. This meaning of wood is destabilized by its substitution with 'plastic and polymorphous substances'. He points to the fact that the categories of 'natural', 'artificial' and 'noble' materials are arbitrary – they have no objective basis – and that the presence of plastics in our experience causes us to supersede such categories. He suggests that the ability of plastics to signify anything and everything has brought about a 'flattening' of the relationships between all materials, natural and artificial, whereby they are 'homogeneous as cultural signs' (p39). For Baudrillard, the malleability of plastics has somehow 'uncovered' the equivalence of all materials, which now have 'exactly the same status as each other', as signs.

It would be a mistake to ignore Baurdillard's and Barthes's acute analysis of the way artificial materials work in contemporary objects, but it would be as much of a mistake to ignore the significance of their materiality. To assume that our perceptions of materials can be reduced to a 'flattened' symbolic register would be to ignore the importance of their physical properties in our interactions with them. Of course we interact with objects and their materials as symbol-reading creatures; but we do this also as embodied beings – we interact in a tactile, emotional, sensual register too, as social beings with the ability to use our interactions with objects as part of our self-presentation. Materials symbolize – they carry cultural 'baggage' – but they also have physical properties which push back at us. It is possible – and Barthes seems to do this – to confuse the cultural significance of materials with their innate properties.

The relationship between the uses that materials have been put to and the properties we then think they have that Baudrillard observes suggests that we do judge materials in terms that are framed by the applications in which we have encountered them. Gay Hawkins points to this in her discussion of how we live with packaging and what we think of its materials. She says of plastic, paper and polystyrene that 'their use in the making of transient objects signifies a finite value, a value waiting to be used up' (2001, p9). It is reasonable to suggest that the identity of materials is to an extent defined by their use; however, it is not reasonable to go as far as to imply that these uses are the end of the story or, if not the end, the most important part of it.

Hawkins argues that to effectively deal with rubbish, and to reach a more sustainable relationship with it, requires that we acknowledge the feelings that it brings up – its emotional impact in relationship to our sense of ourselves. Our usual relationship to rubbish emphasizes separation, what she calls our 'sovereignty' over it (p15), and this appears to be a stable relationship to what we eject, our 'scraps, discards and leftovers'. But a relationship it is, and all relationships can change. Hawkins finishes her article with these words:

> To be moved by waste, to be disturbed by it, is to be open to our own becoming. It is to be able to cultivate a care and sensibility for it that is also at the same time a cultivation of the arts of transience. (2001, p21)

Feelings of disturbance at the packaging waste that flows through our homes are familiar, and these feelings, and the openness and creativity on which packaging re-use depends, derive from a particular type of care and sensibility. In re-use the story of materials continues in people's homes through an 'art of transience'.

Conclusion

This chapter has considered the main groups of packaging materials in turn – wood/card, glass, metal and plastic. In each case, the physical properties of the materials and their application in packaging have been considered in the context of prevailing ideas about them. How packaging works in everyday life can only be grasped fully if both aspects of the 'materiality' of materials are given due attention, the human and the non-human. This approach reflects recent concerns in the study of how people get along with objects in a number of fields over the last 20 or so years, which is beginning to influence how designers think about the results of their work. Materials do not dictate what happens to the objects they comprise; they are not fixed in their effects, but exist as part of the set of relationships between human and non-human actors that develops as a consequence both of material and human 'properties'.

The next chapter considers in detail the human component and identifies the ways that particular orientations and dispositions affect whether and how people may re-use packaging.

Notes

1   The total amount of packaging material waste that is 'wasted', in other words disposed of to landfill, is approximately 5m tonnes – 50 per cent of the 10m tonnes of packaging disposed of each year (the other 50 per cent being recycled).

2   The word 'natural' here is intended to indicate materials that have a vegetable origin – paper, straw, wood. Glass and metal do not fit in this category, and the level of processing that they require in order to be useable suggests that they are less natural. However, the word 'artificial' – as an antonym for 'natural' – is usually found associated with the plastics.

3   Notable exceptions to this general rule in the 20th century include the use of wood during the Second World War for the very successful Mosquito aeroplane made by the De Havilland company for the RAF and its structural use in architecture. Both these applications relied on modern polymer adhesives to produce consistent structural properties in a material that is by nature inconsistent. For a discussion of the development of the Mosquito and architectural applications of laminated timber, see J. E. Gordon's very engaging *New Science of Strong Materials* (1991).

4   Further information about wooden domestic objects can be found in Pinto (1968).

5   See Charles Taylor's (1989, pp368ff) discussion of the importance of the notion of 'inner nature' for modern subjectivity.

6   The common use of paper in Europe dates from its introduction from China in the 8th century. The earliest European paper mills were recorded in Germany in the 14th century, Britain in the late 15th century and the US in the late 17th century (Bolam, 1964).

7   The discovery of glass is credited to the ancient cultures of the Middle East. Macfarlane and Martin (2004) identify the important role that glass and glass-making technology has played in the development of science and civilization, classifying its uses as follows: for beads and jewellery, vessels, windows, mirrors, and in lenses and prisms.

8   An account of the preservation and conservation of the hut at McMurdo Sound is available through the UK and New Zealand Antarctic Heritage Trusts: www.heritage-antarctica.org/aht.htm, accessed January 2009.

9   The UK National Archive records the acquisition of Barringer Wallis and Manners by John Player and Sons: www.nationalarchives.gov.uk/A2A/records.aspx?cat=157-ddpl&cid=-1&Gsm=2008-06-18#-1, accessed February 2009.

10 A number of resources provide a chronology of plastic's history, for example www.plasticsmuseum.org/timeline.html, by the US National Plastics Centre at Leominster, Mass, and www.plastiquarian.com/ind3.htm, by the UK's Plastics Historical Society. Historians and sociologists of technology have also considered plastics, including Bijker (1995), Fenichell (1996), Fisher (2003), Friedel (1983), Katz (1978 and 1984) and Meikle's history of plastics in America (1995). In the mid 20th century, when plastics embodied post-Second World War optimism, this was expressed by writers such as Plastes (1941), Yarsley and Couzens (1942) and Gloag (1945).

11 At the time of writing, a Facebook 'cause' exists called 'Drop the Plastic Bag', with 159,933 members.

12 Archive of the DuPont marketing committee, Hagley Museum and Library, Wilmington, Delaware, Accession Nr 2132, Box 1.

3

Ideas and Values

Introduction

From the emphasis on materials in the previous chapter, we now turn to people. It is worth noting again that to divide our attention to packaging re-use in this way runs counter to the spirit of this book, which tries to emphasize the interaction of all the elements of re-use, to understand the subject in a way that can encompass matter and person, thing and user, object and human. It is the relationships between these things that hold the key to understanding the subject. However, dividing our attention between things and people makes it easier to see the 'anatomy' of packaging re-use, even if this division does not reflect its lived reality. It makes it easier to interpret existing packaging designs and how they may be re-used by different types of people and therefore to facilitate the design of packaging that is more likely to be re-used, but this division is meant to be taken in the integrating spirit of design.

This chapter discusses a number of approaches to thinking about different types of people that are relevant to packaging re-use. Among these are some that have been adopted recently in the UK as part of government initiatives to promote 'pro-environmental' behaviour among consumers. Deriving from the principles of 'social marketing' (Kotler and Lee, 2008), the recent development by Defra (2008) of a model for segmenting the population into different types on the basis of their environmental attitudes and behaviour is discussed as a starting point for understanding how people might respond to packaging designed to facilitate re-use. However, while the packaging re-use that this book is concerned with includes that which responds to efforts from outside agencies such as government, manufacturers and designers to change behaviour, among its central objectives is to understand how people themselves find novel, creative and undirected ways to re-use packaging and to use these insights as the basis for approaches to packaging design that facilitate re-use.

Because people's creative activity is such a significant feature of packaging re-use, a marketing-orientated approach to understanding the human element of packaging re-use is likely to be inadequate. This feature of packaging re-use is also important to bear in mind when thinking about what strategies might be appropriate to change people's behaviour with packaging. Any 'top-down' approach to changing people's behaviour to benefit the environment, such as social marketing campaigns, requires that the behavioural change intended can be clearly defined in advance and that it can be promoted by working with the relevant population segments. While this book does seek to promote a change in behaviour – the re-use of packaging – this objective may be too 'coarse' in its focus to be a useful starting point for a social marketing campaign. Packaging re-use is determined in ways that other types of pro-environmental behavioural may not be. Although, like other pro-environmental behaviour, it requires that the re-use practice fits into people's lives, and this can be facilitated by the design of the packaging, it may always require the inventiveness of individuals to integrate re-used packaging with their everyday routines as well as sufficient commitment from them to do so. While it is easy to think of other pro-environmental behaviours, such as recycling, which have the first two elements – the provision of a recycling system might be an equivalent of the design of a package that facilitates re-use and both require people to adopt appropriate habits and to have appropriate attitudes and expectations of appropriate behaviour – the element that makes packaging re-use distinctive seems to be the degree to which it goes beyond the 'script' provided by a design to draw on people's individual ingenuity and creativity.

This chapter discusses how relevant people's dispositions towards the environment and environmental behaviour are for packaging re-use, drawing from recent work by Defra. This segments the UK population into seven categories, each with a set of attitudes and habits in relation to pro-environmental behaviour (Defra, 2008). The authors' empirical work has demonstrated that much packaging re-use is not motivated by such concerns, however, and is 'indigenous' in that it does not take place in response to information campaigns by government or other agencies. So although this segmentation is interesting, and may describe some people's motivation for some packaging re-use, it does not offer a full picture of the dispositions which may motivate or impede it. To compensate for this, the chapter inspects other ways of thinking about people's dispositions towards their possessions in general and products in particular, particularly in relation to the ways that their material environment of possessions may change. In conventional consumption, a person's ensemble of possessions alters when they acquire a new item, whereas our focus here is on moments when objects that someone already possesses are given a new purpose. This is, however, still a type of 'newness', and the chapter considers a typology of consumers' orientations towards the newness of possessions (Campbell, 1992). Re-use can comprise a moment of creativity in everyday life – a moment of private innovation driven by demands that may be temporary and unique, but which are significant for the person who makes a new connection between object and function. In this respect re-use may have something in common with other more conventional types of innovation, so this chapter introduces ideas about the behaviour of what Von Hippel (1986 and 1988) has called 'lead users'. However, both these sets of ideas also have their limitations for understanding packaging re-use, partly because of its private, non-commercial nature and partly because some of the frameworks they offer simply do not fit with the re-use that can be shown to take place.

Although both these approaches to 'newness' are limited in how much they can inform our understanding of why and how people re-use packaging, these limitations provide useful starting points for thinking about what factors are relevant. Campbell identifies the importance for some consumers of the pristine appearance of their possessions as a motivation for acquiring new ones. The chapter relates the feelings about objects that this 'pristinian' attitude implies to the discussion of materials in Chapter 2, noting the strong significance to re-use of feelings about objects – we are not inclined to re-use packaging that we feel negatively towards, particularly if the re-use is around food and the negative feelings are in our gut. These feelings about the materiality of packaging are set in the context of ways of thinking about how we respond to different qualities in the 'stuff' of packaging – its physical materials – as well as ways of thinking about cultural patterns that give this stuff significance. Ideas about people are integrated again with ideas about things through a discussion of how we come to have particular feelings about particular things.

This integration is followed through in a series of examples of re-use that indicate different motivations for extending the life of packaging. These include inventive responses to physical needs, a desire to save waste by being thrifty that has environmental benefits but may not be motivated by them, and a desire to demonstrate good taste in the arrangement of objects in the home and in the garden. Of these instances of re-use, those that happen in places where things are on display can be understood as part of the performance of the self through objects, drawing from Goffman. The chapter ends by noting that some of the differences between these examples relate to their different settings as well as the motivation of the people doing the re-use. This leads on to the next chapter, which considers how the location of objects in the spaces of the home influences re-use practices.

Types of people – Influences, Attitudes and Segmentations

It seems reasonable to suppose that people who are minded to transcend the design of a pack to re-use it share some characteristics. At a basic level, re-using packaging may reflect what psychologist Ives Kendrick (1942, p40) saw as an inherent feature of all human beings' relationship to the material world. He called this 'instinct to master', an 'inborn drive to do and to learn how to do', which underlies our relationship with objects. While a drive to master the environment may be one aspect of the human psyche that leads us to re-use packaging, it may be too abstract an idea to be directly helpful in designing to promote re-use. Cultural factors are more obviously useful

– a person's attitudes to environmental sustainability as well as the degree to which they are motivated by thrift and social 'face' are likely to affect whether they think of re-using packaging. It would be a mistake, however, to think of such factors as completely separate from the possibly instinctive willingness to take the 'hands-on' approach to artefacts that Kendrick identifies. Because a good deal of the packaging that enters the home does so associated with food, decisions about whether to re-use it, and ideas about what are acceptable uses for it, have immediate connections to our sensitivities to hygiene and cleanliness, which we are aware of through our emotions. Like all our emotions, these feelings about what it is appropriate to do with packaging have both cultural and instinctive components.

Dispositions to re-use, or not, are likely to be influenced by a range of early life experiences. For UK adults these have been mediated by various influences, ranging from formal government information campaigns to a positive emphasis on 'hands-on' craft activities in schools and the mass media. Alongside the experience of scarcity and poverty in the period immediately following the Second World War, the influence is still evident of the UK government's 'make do and mend' campaign, which was publicised by a series of Board of Trade pamphlets offering tips for extending the life of clothes and household items. So too is the influence of an ethic of hands-on engagement with material in the entertainment directed at children in the late 20th century. This is exemplified by *Blue Peter*'s 'makes', in which trusted adult role models have routinely re-used packaging to create toys and models for over four decades. Other programming for children may in a less obvious way have also led people to be disposed to re-use packaging, from Tony Hart in the 1960s to *Smart* and *Art Attack* on UK television in the present. When talking about the ways they re-use packaging, research participants readily referred to the *Blue Peter* tag 'here's one I made earlier' or used the Second World War slogan 'make do and mend' as a way to explain their actions and give them a positive gloss. However, these influences may not always have a positive effect on re-use, and there were some participants for whom they had distinctly negative associations of want and poverty (Shipton, 2007).

Relationships to the Environment; People and Packaging

Whatever the early influences on an individual's attitudes to waste, thrift and making things, their attitudes to the environment are likely to be a significant determinant on whether they are minded to re-use packaging. Environmental attitudes have been the subject of considerable research associated with campaigns to change consumers' behaviour, and this has led to attempts to segment the population in respect of attitudes and behaviour related to the environment. In the UK, Marks and Spencer's 'Plan A' strategy to promote and facilitate pro-environmental behaviour among their customers has worked out what people's generalized attitudes are to such behaviour. In a 2008 review of the first year of Plan A, Marks and Spencer published the results of consumer research which segmented the population into four groups in respect of these generalized attitudes. According to this segmentation, 24 per cent of people feel detached from environmental issues – the 'not my problem' group; 38 per cent belong to the 'what's the point' group – they have some concern with the issues but can't see that their actions will have a positive effect; 27 per cent are in the 'if it's easy' group, prepared to change their behaviour if it takes no significant effort; and 11 per cent of people are committed to changing their behaviour in environmentally positive ways and fit the 'green crusader' group (Marks and Spencer, 2008).

Marks and Spencer's efforts to change their customers' behaviour fits the 'social marketing' approach, where marketers act as change agents seeking to influence people towards 'good' behaviours (Kotler and Lee, 2008). Andreasen (2002, p296) gives the following definition of social marketing:

The application of commercial marketing technologies to the analysis, planning, execution and evaluation of programmes designed to influence the voluntary behaviour of target audiences in order to improve their personal welfare and that of society.

It seems less appropriate to think in these terms about packaging re-use that occurs spontaneously, however, since it takes place in the absence of government or other social marketing efforts to change behaviour. It is opportunistic and comes out of the population, rather than being imposed on it. The proposition of this book is that design can work with this spontaneous consumer activity and embed 'affordances' for re-use into packaging. The focus of this chapter is on understanding the consumer attitudes and actions that may make those affordances relevant and result in a pack being re-used.

Here the word 'affordance' is meant in the sense coined by perception psychologist James Jerome Gibson (1977 and 1979) to describe aspects of the environment that people recognize and find to fit their purposes. The concept allows for aspects of the man-made environment to be designed to fit purposes that can be predicted – to function in particular ways, to provide predictable affordances. Crucially for this discussion, the concept also allows for a process in which people discover aspects of the world that fit their intentions – that allow them to do what they want to do – but which have not necessarily been put there deliberately to fit those intentions. The concept of affordance allows for 'open' objects that can be interpreted and reinterpreted by different people or groups of people. To use the terminology about function introduced in Chapter 1, the affordances that people find in objects may simply be side-effects of their 'proper function' and arise due to the 'system' that they are part of – it may be the place that a piece of packaging ends up that causes us to change our behaviour towards it, rather than the efforts of its designers.

In the absence of coordinated social marketing efforts to change behaviour and packaging re-use, the only available agent of change is the packaging design itself. There are examples of packs designed with specific further uses in mind, such as Heineken's WOBO or World Bottle – a beer bottle designed to be used as a brick when empty. This was invented in 1963 by brewer Alfred Heineken, working with architect John Habraken in response to a need he saw for a cheap building material (Pawley, 1975). The design was not supported by the Heineken Company, however, and even if it had been, the 'closed' nature of the designed-in re-use is likely to have limited its effectiveness. Although the potential it has for re-use is evident in its form, no system was developed to support its secondary function. Also, the form is 'closed' in that the only obvious re-use for the WOBO is as a brick. The WOBO may indeed be closed in two ways. The fact that it has this re-use designed into it so strongly may mean both that it is physically impossible to re-use it in other ways and that the marked influence of this affordance for re-use on its form means that it is more difficult to see other ways of re-using it than is the case for a regular bottle.

The way packaging is conventionally designed means it is intended to be an agent of behaviour change only in respect of consumers' product choices – to persuade them of the safety, convenience and brand values of the pack's contents over its competitors, rather than to change their behaviour for the common good. Sometimes aspects of a design may appeal to consumers' environmental concern or sense of responsibility, and seek to promote 'good' behaviours, but given the commercial imperatives that are the strongest influence on packaging, designs like this may primarily be intended to help to make a sale rather than to make a significant environmental difference. For example, some food packages have card and plastic components that can be separated from each other. Just as designing a bottle as a brick does not guarantee it will be used as one, these design elements may or may not produce the desirable behaviour of separating materials in the waste stream, but they may lessen anxiety about buying packaged food among individuals who are susceptible to it and therefore may promote sales.

A complicating factor in the relationship between consumers' attitudes and their consequent actions with packaging is the acknowledged fact that knowing that a particular way of acting has negative consequences may not produce the change in behaviour that the knowledge might imply. This 'value–action gap' is discussed by Andrew Darnton in a review of models that have been developed to help to design programmes to change behaviours, particularly in people's consumption habits. Quoting Monroe, this is the conundrum of 'why, if people care about polar bears, they still drive SUVs' (Monroe, 2006, quoted in Darnton, 2008, p10). Despite this puzzle, it is still possible to link actions to values to some extent, and in the UK Defra has recently developed a way of segmenting the population on the basis of their actions and attitudes to environmental issues that can be applied to a range of different specific behaviours.

While Marks and Spencer's model defined four types of person, Defra's Environmental Behaviour Model (2008) splits the UK population into seven segments. This segmentation model is relevant to packaging re-use, as it concentrates on people's behaviour as consumers, much of which centres on the household. It is intended to inform actions to bring about behaviour change through social marketing interventions and was developed with this in mind as part of Defra's Sustainable Consumption and Production programme.[1] It seeks to capture attitudes that transcend any particular behaviour and that reflect an individual's overall orientation towards the environment. As Defra put it, the model 'divides the public into seven clusters each sharing a distinct set of attitudes and beliefs towards the environment, environmental issues and behaviours' (2008, p8).

The characteristics of people in the segments range from 'strongly moti-vated to act in a pro-environmental manner and able to do so' in Segment 1, through 'motivated by thrift and therefore may take pro-environmental actions but not because of their effect on the environment' in Segment 2, to 'little concern and unlikely to act in a pro-environmental manner even if able to' in Segment 7 (see box below). The proportions of the population who fall into each of the groups is significant, in that approaching a fifth of people have 'positive green' attitudes and beliefs and about the same proportion are 'disengaged' from the issues. The research on which the segmentation model was based discovered some significant barriers to pro-environmental behaviour that cut across the segmentation model, such as the fact that nearly a quarter of the population consider that their actions do not affect climate change and the belief that one individual's actions cannot make a difference to problems that are global in scope (Defra, 2008, p35).

Box 3.1 *Character quotations for the seven Defra environmental behaviour segments*

Segment 1: 'Positive greens' (18%)

'I think we need to do some things differently to tackle climate change. I do what I can and I feel bad about the rest.'

Segment 2: 'Waste watchers' (12%)

'Waste not, want not – that's important. You should live life thinking about what you're doing and using.'

Segment 3: 'Concerned consumers' (14%)

'I think I do more than a lot of people. Still, going away is important, I'd find that hard to give up... well, I wouldn't, so carbon offsetting would make me feel better.'

Segment 4: 'Sideline supporters' (14%)

'I think climate change is a big problem for us. I suppose I don't think much about how much water or electricity I use, and I forget to turn things off. I'd like to do a bit more.'

Segment 5: 'Cautious participants' (14%)

'I do a couple of things to help the environment. I'd really like to do more... well, as long as I saw others were.'

Segment 6: 'Stalled starters' (10%)

'I don't know much about climate change. I can't afford a car so I use public transport. I'd like a car though.'

Segment 7: 'Honestly disengaged' (18%)

'Maybe there'll be an environmental disaster, maybe not. Makes no difference to me; I'm just living my life the way I want to.'

Source: Defra (2008)

Although it may not be possible to neatly apply the social marketing approach embedded in Defra's Sustainable Consumption and Production programme to packaging re-use, the details of some aspects of the segmentation model may help us to see how to promote it, particularly segment-specific approaches to bringing about changes in people's behaviour (Defra, 2008, pp51ff). Some segments of the population are both minded to act and able to. Segments 1, 3 and 4, in which people have appropriate attitudes and mainly act on them, are therefore likely to respond most readily to behaviour-change campaigns. Segments 2 and 5 have some appropriate attitudes, but are sometimes blocked from taking action. Of these, Segment 2 – the 12 per cent of the population who are 'waste watchers' – may be motivated to re-use packaging because of a desire to be thrifty and avoid wasting materials. As well as being relatively conservative in their outlook, members of this group tend to be older. It is tempting to assume that it is in the current generation of people of this age group that the 'make do and mend' ethic discussed above persists most strongly, but being motivated by thrift is independent of historical circumstances and is apparently a feature of this later life stage in all generations (Defra, 2008, pp54–55). If thriftiness does align with packaging re-use, then a propensity to re-use packaging may be something that people grow into as they get older. While the qualitative nature of our research means it is not possible to measure whether frequency of packaging re-use correlates with life stage, it identified people of all ages who re-use packaging, with apparently different motivations.

While these segmentation models provide insights into people's behaviour, there are limits to their application in promoting packaging re-use through design. The factors that determine whether or not an individual re-uses a pack certainly overlap with those on which Defra's segmentation is based, but a propensity to re-use packaging is as likely to be motivated by habit or immediate pressing need as by a general orientation to environmental sustainability. Our research has also demonstrated that significant barriers to packaging re-use include factors that may not be relevant in other types of pro-environmental behaviour, for instance attitudes to newness and to hygiene.

Newness and Invention

This section maintains the focus on people, using ideas from innovation theory and studies of consumption to suggest ways of thinking about how re-use comes about. The spontaneous, inventive and private nature of re-use means that, like the population segmentation model discussed above, these ideas give only partial insights into its characteristics. However, they are particularly helpful in identifying aspects of people's relationship to objects in general and new objects in particular that may reduce the likelihood that packaging will be re-used. This helps to show more clearly what lies behind the re-use that does take place.

Is re-using packaging a type of innovation? 'Open-loop' re-use always means finding a purpose for a piece of packaging other than the one intended by its designer – even simply using an object such as a jam jar to store something other than jam gives it a new function. This is self-evident, but points to the fact that re-use always consists of some type of invention – and inventions maybe classed as innovations if they are widely adopted. Even if the inventive aspect of re-use is played down, as it is when it is called 're-purposing', some inventive content remains. Even in the simplest examples of re-use the object has a new function, a new affordance has been spotted in it, although its physical arrangement may not be altered. For this reason, and continuing in the spirit of this chapter in seeking to characterize people who may have a propensity to re-use packaging, it is useful to review some ideas from innovation theory. Eric Von Hippel identified what he calls 'lead users', who relate to objects in an unusual way and can see beyond conventional expectations to develop them in new directions.

The sense in which a re-used object can be thought of as new is not clear. Although its function may be new to it and to its owner, this is a particular type of newness, without the usual cachet of a pristine object newly acquired. It is not clear what the implications of this are for people's preparedness to re-use packaging. To cast light on this, the discussion will turn to ideas about people's relationship to new objects as consumers developed by cultural sociologist Colin Campbell, referring on the way to the work of Mary Douglas. Campbell's discussion of different orientations to newness that may affect people's disposition towards acquiring new goods encompasses the influence of a person's existing, no longer new, possessions. While it makes sense to think about newness in trying to understand how people put packaging to a new use, the raw material they employ in doing this is not new. Re-use is the transformation of something used into something with a new function, but the object itself may remain the same – it is certainly not new in the sense we have become accustomed to as modern consumers; it is renewed rather than new.[2] For this reason, it is appropriate to consider what influence this 'used-ness' might have on people's readiness to re-use packaging.

Discussing why people desire new things, Colin Campbell (1992) identified three different types of relationship to 'newness', which he sums up as three types of people. Two of these types are not obviously relevant to packaging re-use – these are people motivated to consume new products because they are novel – in other words different from those they are familiar with – or because they are technical improvements over the old. But Campbell also identifies a third type of person for whom it is important to have new things to replace possessions that have become, as he puts it, 'contaminated' by use. Campbell calls this type of person a 'pristinian' – they like to maintain their material environment in a pristine state and will acquire new goods for this reason. Because of the special, perhaps restricted, nature of the 'newness' in re-used packaging, there are only indirect connections between packaging re-use and Campbell's discussion, but nonetheless it helps to indicate some of the special features of re-use. Re-using a piece of packaging seems on the face of it not to fit with any of the three motivations for consumption that Campbell identifies, because the re-used object is not new, only its use is. A desire for the types of newness we are familiar with cannot be satisfied in re-using a bag, a box or a plastic container.

But Campbell's typology assumes that consumers have a relatively passive relationship to consumption. This assumption does not hold true in some types of conventional consumption and by definition cannot apply when people re-use packaging. What has been called 'user innovation' has been described in fields as diverse as computer software, medical instruments, outdoor clothing, sports equipment and mountain bikes,[3] and demonstrates that at least some consumers are not passive, but have a very engaged 'hands-on' relationship with their possessions. The creativity and preparedness to engage with objects to change their function that is necessary to packaging re-use may have more in common with user innovation than with the conventional sequence of dissatisfaction with a possession and its replacement with a new item that Campbell discusses.

Packaging re-users are neither consumers nor producers in the conventional sense. They are likely to have a closer relationship with a piece of packaging once it is re-used than they had with it when it was following its normal course through the home. Their re-used object is from somewhere particular rather than from the anonymous space of production – they have rescued it from its destiny as waste by exercising some creativity in its consumption. However, our familiarity with the conventional life-story of packaging may in itself inhibit its re-use for another purpose. Von Hippel (1988, pp102ff) identifies the difficulty that users have in identifying new possibilities for objects. As he puts it, 'Familiarity with existing product attributes and uses interferes with an individual's ability to conceive of novel attributes and uses.'

Von Hippel reviews studies of problem-solving as evidence for a tendency for people not to innovate – not to see new possibilities in existing objects. He cites a 1945 study by Duncker which noted that people tend not to see an alternative use for an object if they have recently seen it fulfilling its conventional purpose. This 'functional fixedness' may also apply to packaging, but the fact that some packaging does get re-used suggests that this fixedness is balanced to some extent by a tendency to see opportunities and 'openings' in familiar objects. Some people are able to see beyond the conventional life-story of packs. And some designs, those 'open' designs which have built into them potential affordances for further uses, may actively work against this fixedness.

Von Hippel notes that there is a strong relationship between particular configurations of objects and existing practices – what he calls 'usage patterns'. The ways in which relationships between patterns of life and packaging affect its re-use will be discussed in more detail in Chapters 4 and 5 in the context of the domestic spaces in which much packaging re-use takes place. These firmly entrenched patterns mean that people need to work out for themselves how a new product might change the patterns of life, the practices, with which they are familiar. Von Hippel talks about this process of exploring new ways of living with objects as a quite rational process, in which the relationship between usage patterns and new or modified objects is clear:

> *Users must invent or select the new (to them) usage patterns that the proposed new product makes possible for the first time and then evaluate the utility of the product in these patterns. (1988, p103)*

The language used here suggests that user-consumers do this in a somewhat detached, rationalizing manner. But a user 'evaluating the utility' of a new product may not capture the situation that people are in when re-using packaging, which is likely to be more physically engaged – hands on. In an echo of the lack of relevance of a social marketing approach to re-use, this may be a consequence of the fact that Von Hippel defines his lead user as relating to objects in a conventional market context. For instance, he ascribes them these two defining characteristics:

1 *Lead users face needs that will be general in a marketplace, but they face them months or years before the bulk of that marketplace encounters them; and*
2 *Lead users are positioned to benefit significantly by obtaining a solution to those needs.* *(p107)*

These characteristics do not apply to a person who re-uses packaging, because re-use tends to take place in private and to be a response to a relatively private need that is identified by an individual in their everyday life. Though others may very well have similar needs, they do not exist in relation to a classically conceived market where consumers make rational choices between alternative ways to spend their money. The financial element in re-use is likely to be an incentive to save money, rather than choosing how to spend it. Also, because the creativity that exists in re-use generally takes place in the private spaces of the home, the comparison between alternatives that is a feature of markets is not possible in quite the same way.

To think of someone who re-uses packaging as a *lead* user also implies that others will adopt their innovative re-use. This may happen if the re-use is public and it is observed by others or if it is disseminated in some other way, but re-use in the domestic setting that has a close fit with the texture of an individual's life patterns and habits may never be observed and not lead anyone anywhere. A tendency for such re-use to be private is built into its character because of its location and may be reinforced by people's feelings about doing it. To be motivated by thrift, with its connotations of miserliness, is not necessarily something that people will want others to know about – a degree of coyness about their re-use habits was evident among the partici-pants in the authors' research.[4]

It might be possible to create some sort of market in re-use that inno-vators could lead, encouraging the diffusion of ideas and practices, but this would require some intervention to allow individuals' innovations to diffuse to others. Such interventions could be collective if they used the networked communication that is available online – a very large number of online groups exist that discuss and exchange knowledge about all sorts of arcane subjects, from French-horn making to taxi driving (Fisher, 2008; Ross, 2007). However, there is a spontaneous desire to exchange knowledge among people who engage with these subjects which seems to be absent in respect of packaging re-use. Recycling, on the other hand, inspires a similar desire – at the time of writing there are 16,216 Yahoo! groups related to recycling, but none to pack-aging re-use. Given people's desire to exchange information, this stands to be a very effective way of promoting packaging re-use, though one potentially negative consequence of this sort of communication would be if it served to 'fix' re-use into a set of recipes. This might discourage exactly the type of independent inventiveness that the most compelling examples of re-use seem to rely on, such as those discussed below.

Von Hippel's work is useful for understanding re-use to the extent that it acknowledges the relationship between objects and practices, but whereas in his view the 'fixedness' of habits and practices would likely inhibit re-use and promote disposal, it is possible to see these same practices intimately bound up with decisions *to re-use* as well as decisions to discard. The way we live with objects is not governed only by rationality, or only by habit, or only by the objects we encounter, for that matter. Recent work in sociology has unpacked how complex networks of relationships between people and objects become embedded, come to seem normal, and how they may change. Elizabeth Shove (2003) has identified the ways in which our ideas about normal standards for indoor environments for living and working in have fed into and been influ-enced by the development and increasing use of air-conditioning systems, as well as the way our having washing machines and plentiful hot water for showering has been tied up with changing habits of washing our bodies and our clothes as well as changes in how we feel about both. In a similar vein, Harvey Molotch (2003) has analysed a number of different types of object, including toasters, toilets and computers, to demonstrate how their current form is the result of people in many different roles as well as diverse economic, technical, social and cultural forces.

The factors that influence someone to re-use packaging are much more local, more private, and the consequences probably more slight than is the case for the highly embedded and widely distributed 'compounds' of objects, feelings and habits that Shove and Molotch discuss. However, although someone who re-uses a piece of packaging operates alone, it would be a mistake to think that they take the decision to do so in isolation – they work with a repertoire of knowledge, expectations, feelings and conventions, as well as with the material reality of the object itself. As we saw in Chapter 2, materials have their own repertoires of abilities – they will do some things but not others – as well as their own sets of associations, their own stories. Similarly, people work with the degree to which designs embody potential affordances for re-use; objects have their own repertoires of potential performances – their designs allow them to do some things but not others – and they invoke certain associations. Affordances are social and cultural as much as physical (Heft, 1989; Costall, 1995).

Of the human and non-human factors just mentioned, it is perhaps our feelings about objects that we are most aware of. This register of our everyday existence is acknowledged by some sociologists as a significant feature of the practices that we engage in[5] – we do what we do with objects partly because of what we feel about them. In the 'pristinian' consumer Colin Campbell describes an aspect of our practices with objects that is clearly based on feelings and which is certainly significant in packaging re-use. Individuals with pristinian tendencies may apply different standards to different types of possessions – front-stage ones may be treated differently to back-stage ones – but someone for whom cleanliness is important may be challenged particularly by rescuing some types of packaging from waste to re-use them. Their desire for perfection in their possessions is likely to create a need to be able to thoroughly clean packaging before it can be re-used.

We feel emotions; we do not think them. When we remark on sweaty palms, a trembling stomach, a tight head, a thumping heart, we can say to ourselves we are feeling an emotion. They can seem to be entirely restricted to our physical being and indeed to be in conflict with and sometimes obscure our thinking self. Although this is how they seem, and it strongly influences some ways of understanding them scientifically, there are strong arguments which suggest that emotions have a significant cultural dimension, that to an extent they are things that we do as much as things that we have. If this is the case – and historical studies that show the ways that emotions like grief have changed over time suggest it is – then to understand a feeling we have to understand the culture that the person experiencing it inhabits. We will consider this aspect of our practices with packaging – our feelings about whether or not they are contaminated – to open up the cultural dimension of its re-use.[6]

Hygiene and Disposability

Standards of cleanliness and hygiene change through time, along with patterns of expectation about our surroundings and the technical ways we have at our disposal to interact with them. The anthropologist Mary Douglas (1966) famously identified the relationship between ideas of hygiene and cleanliness and cultural patterns, noting that there is no such thing as 'absolute' dirt, only 'matter out of place'. Whatever the prevailing notions about dirt, they strongly influence our behaviour. Elizabeth Shove (2003) has shown how ideas about normal standards of cleanliness the quantity of alongside configurations of technologies and habits to influence the quantity of resources our everyday practices consume. For instance, many people now have a strong feeling they should shower at least once every day and have clean clothes to wear each time they do. This has a very significant environmental impact through the water and energy consumption that results from washing ourselves and our clothes (Allwood et al, 2006) and is in the end motivated by feelings – we want to feel clean; we don't like to feel dirty – and these feelings are determined by our culture.

Chapter 2 discussed the associations people have with different packaging materials and the consequences these have for whether a pack will be re-used. The degree to which a surface is 'fused' – glass compared to wood, for instance – plays on expectations of hygiene and cleanliness and influences people's willingness to use these materials to contain food. The extent to which it is possible to completely remove the product from its pack is therefore relevant to whether it is considered suitable to re-use. Just as ideas about dirt are specific to a time and place, we have become accustomed to classifying packaging as rubbish because of the material culture of our times. The history of the rubbish industry coincides with the history of urbanization in the West, as Heather Rogers (2005) explains in her critical account of the subject, and our habits are a product of that history. Rogers tells a story of institutions and public health campaigns, but this is also a history of ideas. Gavin Lucas (2002) gives an account of these ideas, suggesting that the principles of thrift and hygiene as they have played out in our domestic arrangements have been important factors in getting us to our current situation of finding nothing strange in treating packaging as waste. As Lucas puts it, developing Douglas's principle, 'rubbish is what it is, because of its position in the classificatory schemes connected to practices of hygiene' (2002, p8).

Lucas summarizes the move in the early 20th century from re-usable to disposable packaging. This was partly a shift in materials, from expensive, locally produced and therefore re-usable glass/ceramic to cheaper glass and paper/card, but it was also closely related to what he calls the 'new discourses of personal hygiene' of the early 20th century, which affected not only the products associated with kitchen and bathroom, but also the design of those spaces themselves, as Lupton and Miller describe (1992). These new packages offered consumers cleanliness *because of* their disposability – the fact that they were made to be thrown away meant that every newly purchased item was newly made and therefore clean. Disposability guarantees cleanliness. Lucas also notes an economic dimension to disposability, whereby the risk that early commentators saw of the cost of disposable packaging being a disincentive to consumption is neutralized by the expectation that it will be thrown away, classed as valueless even at the point of purchase.

So in our times, to re-use packaging means overcoming an assumption that once it has been used it is irrevocably contaminated. Also, the assumption that packaging is worthless may be a barrier to its re-use, because to re-use something is to give it some value. These disincentives to re-use reinforce each other, but they are balanced by a persisting ethic of thrift, expressed in the behaviour segmentation described above. Lucas points out, though, that these two sets of ideas are not simple opposites, because of the complexity that is characteristic of dispossession – he suggests that 'in the general economy of the household ... shedding off possessions can be as complex a process as acquiring them' (2002, p17). He shows that dispossession habits vary with different types of object, citing an American study of the way people dispose of their possessions which suggested that large items – fridges, furniture and so on – are less likely to be thrown away and are stored, sold or re-used in the same family. Clearly, though, a great deal of packaging *is* thrown away and enters the waste stream. Disposal is built into its design. So it is necessary to understand ideas about waste – when an item becomes waste rather than a possession; when and how its path to the bin can be arrested or reversed – to understand re-use.

The moment of dispossession – when an item is got rid of for good; the point at which its owner feels thoroughly alienated from it – is not clear-cut. Even in the bin items retain some of their owner's loyalty, as is shown by the protectiveness people feel over the contents of their own rubbish. The ethics of consumption mean we fear judgement on the contents of our bin as we might fear judgement on the contents of our supermarket trolley. Lucas makes the welcome point that studies of consumption need to take the processes of dispossession as seriously as processes of acquisition, adopting Marxist language of appropriation and alienation to consider the ways in which dispossession happens and can be delayed by, for instance, the hoarding of items that may otherwise be consigned to the bin. He suggests that people are more likely to hoard objects in which they have more emotional and financial investment. Although this rings true, in our research we have observed people storing packaging in border zones between use and disposal, which suggests that hoarding is not limited to objects of intrinsically high value.

Michael Thompson (1979) suggests that the defining feature of rubbish is that it is 'deconstituted'. Having crossed the border into this state, items lose their identity and value; they become part of an undifferentiated mess in a bin or landfill. Although our work has shown that packaging is quite often held back for a time from crossing this border, in its conventional life-cycle packaging crosses it in only one direction; it is briefly valued as a useful container for goods and then classified as waste. After being briefly 'de-alienated' from packaging when we recognize a brand and buy goods, after a brief period of possession we become alienated from it again and it becomes undifferentiated waste. While it may seem unlikely that the disinclination to dispose of larger items to waste mentioned above would apply to such everyday stuff as used packaging, the authors' research has demonstrated that people are quite commonly disinclined to be alienated even from these objects. The domestic spaces discussed in subsequent chapters quite often contain 'twilight zones' in which packaging objects linger with what identity and value they have preserved, their disposal deferred, waiting for possible re-use. These twilight zones stop packaging crossing the border into undifferentiated rubbish. From this discussion of ideas of hygiene, thrift and disposability, attention now turns to some of the ways in which relationships between the properties of things and the make-up of people can interact in particular instances of re-use, to relate some of the ideas introduced in Chapters 1 and 2 to ideas about people and their dispositions towards dispossession and re-use.

Actions and Performances

I make things out of cereal packets – templates for when I'm sewing and so on. Strange but true – I don't share this with people.

I've been known to use tissue boxes to keep things in, but please don't tell anyone – it drives my husband mad.

These two quotes indicate that people's relationship with re-use can be complex. Re-using packaging may not be something they want to be known for, and a disposition that leads them to re-use packaging may conflict with what others feel are appropriate actions to take with packaging. The previous discussion of the dispositions that people have which may affect whether they re-use packaging has identified as probable factors in re-use aspects of individuals' background and experiences that may play out in their attitudes to the environment, as well as their relationship to standards of hygiene and ethics of thrift. So apart from the implication of stinginess that might go along with re-using packaging, mentioned above, there may also be issues to do with hygiene in re-using objects that are considered disposable in part for reasons of hygiene. While for some people re-using packaging is a habit with potentially negative connotations, other instances of re-use are more publicly displayed. Returning to the concepts from Goffman, introduced in Chapter 1, this chapter will finish by thinking about some examples of packaging re-use which may comprise the 'performance' of positive attitudes towards re-use. These examples can be considered as instances where people publicly display their re-used packaging as part of the performance of what Russel Belk (1988) has called the 'extended self' of possessions in the home.

Goffman (1951) described the role that symbols play in communicating social status – an individual's class position. He acknowledges that status goes along with values, suggesting that in symbolizing group membership, status symbols can express 'the point of view, the style of life and the cultural values of the person' (p295). Just as in principle any object or behaviour can symbolize cultural values, so the behaviour of re-using packaging may be allied to 'pro-environmental' values. The patterns of behaviour that go along with the Defra population segments broadly map across the social classes – Segment 1 is mainly populated by socio-economic groups AB and Segment 6 is made up of 50 per cent DE. Communication to others of a person's relative environmental commitment can therefore be taken to be equivalent to the communication of class described by Goffman and may be accomplished through re-using packaging.

To the extent that packaging re-use derives from commitment to environmental values – and this is by no means the only motivation behind it – this is likely to be important in the symbolic 'work' that it does as part of the presentation of the extended self. Re-use does not necessarily have a relationship to environmental ethics or to ethics of thrift, because it may simply be the result of habit or opportunistic problem-solving. But it seems safe to assume that it does often have this connection. It follows that the display of re-used packaging in the home will comprise the performance of this aspect of some people's self-identity – possibly those in the population segments identified by Defra as more 'pro-environmental'.

People re-use packaging in various spaces in the home, including the kitchen, living spaces and garden, spaces that are discussed in more detail in the next chapter. All of these spaces now count as 'front-stage' settings for the performance of self through objects, though this has not always been the case. The evolution of the kitchen from quasi-factory to a living space in which the same level of aesthetic judgement is necessary as is appropriate for more obviously front-stage areas took place over the 20th century and is to a large extent complete. Irene Cieraad describes this evolution of the kitchen into a space which is increasingly integrated into the rest of what becomes, as she puts it, 'one large homely domain' (2002, p275) where the extended self is on display. In a similar way, gardens now qualify for treatment as extensions of the indoor space, functioning as what Gross and Lane call an 'external feature of the home', that is 'an element of personal territory' (2007, p227). The evolution and current status of these domestic spaces will be fully explored in the next chapter, but the following examples show packaging re-used in all these spaces, for their physical function and for the Goffmanesque presentation of the self.

Figure 3.1 shows packaging re-used in a garden – beer bottles buried neck downwards to make a line that demarcates a path from a border. The physical properties of their material makes them suitable for this task: their fused surface means the bottles will remain unchanged for some time and it will be possible to clean them and maintain their appearance. Glass has some of the elemental permanence of other materials that are conventionally characteristic of gardens. Re-using them to make a path edge in this way is reminiscent of the re-use that was designed into the Heineken World Bottle, discussed above, though the significant difference here is that that these bottles were not designed with this future use in mind – rather they were designed to suit a context where such bottles are cheap enough and light enough that they are used only once.

The affordance for this purposeful arrangement exists in the bottles' standard design – the design is 'open' enough to allow it. Whether or not the householder themselves spotted this affordance and had the idea of using the bottles to create a division between path and flower bed, there is creativity inherent in the decision to do so since it is a subversion of the 'proper' function of the bottles to be treated as waste having been used once. Creativity is characteristic of people's relationship with gardens, as Gross and Lane (2007) note. Mark Francis (1990), in an edited collection that includes a representative selection of 1980s academic work on gardens, puts this creativity into the context of the other roles that gardens have in people's lives. He stresses that gardens serve as spaces for contemplation, freedom and retreat, and that they are created through experiment and creativity to reflect their owners' personalities.

It is now conventional in the UK to recycle glass packaging – most individuals are aware of recycling as an environmental 'good' and if asked will assert that they recycle their waste. Glass recycling is so prevalent that it is quite

Figure 3.1 Beer bottles used for garden edging

Source: Authors

likely that someone who re-uses glass bottles in this way does it knowing that this re-use is an alternative to disposing of the bottles either through council collection or by taking them to a collection site. Re-using the bottles in this way may constitute the sort of public display of pro-environmental attitudes suggested above, combined perhaps with a display of ingenuity and inventiveness. Either of these motivations is close enough to self-identity that it is possible to think of this re-use in Goffman's terms – the garden is the setting for this performance of environmentalist creativity, with the re-used bottles serving as props.

Figure 3.2 also shows packaging re-used in a garden, this time a large plastic water bottle is serving as a temporary cloche over lettuces in a vegetable garden. This has required that the packaging is altered – the bottom has been cut out of the bottle to fit it over the growing plants to give them a protected environment, creating a new object. There may be some similarities with the previous example in the ways that this re-use fits with the characteristics of the person who found this purpose for the water bottle – they were likely motivated by a desire to save waste by re-using a bulky piece of

Figure 3.2 Large water bottle re-used as a bell cloche

Source: Authors

packaging that is almost as awkward to dispose of by recycling as through the waste bin. This action could have had a pro-environmental 'gloss' and therefore be seen to some extent as a public performance of this aspect of their self-identity. However, for all that vegetable growing does now feature as part of some gardens for decorative effect, it still may be differentiated from the more aesthetically motivated aspects of gardens – the activities of growing flowers and growing vegetables have different stories attached and the spaces in which they are done follow different patterns, which are explored in the next chapter. If it is part of a performance of self-identity through objects, this example of re-use perhaps demonstrates the inventiveness of the gardener and their commitment to results, rather than a desire to use objects and materials to decorative/aesthetic effect to establish the garden as an extension of the house. The fact that this cloche is still a water bottle – even down to the presence of the label and the handle – whereas the beer bottles in Figure 3.1 were used as a building element in the architecture of the garden means the water bottle remains a separate and separable item, an invention, a device rather than a building component.

The differences between flower gardens and vegetable gardens may account for some of the differences between these two examples – the aesthetic requirements of the two types of space are different and provide different sets of limits and motivations on re-use. Re-use in both settings can be thought of as front-stage performance, in that the re-used objects remain on display – possibly more so in the vegetable garden than in the more private space of the domestic garden – but the content of the performance is different. The concept of the 'field' that Pierre Bourdieu (1984) uses to distinguish between taste judgements in different settings may be an apt way of thinking about these differences. A vegetable garden is productive, whereas a flower garden is contemplative. The values that go along with vegetable gardening are strongly influenced by prevailing ideas of nature; the desirable human relationships with the latter can be expressed through the choice to use 'organic' practices, or to use more modern techniques of horticulture. It is possible that vegetable growing that is influenced by the former set of values opens the possibility for a more casual approach to the aesthetic dimension of vegetable gardens and the consequent display of creative efforts to re-use packaging such as the example in Figure 3.2, since both connect to an environmentalist ethic. A plastic container re-used with its label might be out of place in a flower garden, but not in a vegetable garden, and particularly not in one influenced by organic practices.

Staying with the emphasis in this chapter on the aspects of people that influence re-use, these two examples indicate different motivations for re-use that are bound up in the standards and values that go along with their settings and which are experienced in what 'feels right' in each place – the knowledge of the practices of vegetable and flower growing that is evident in emotions. The care with which the decorative effect of the re-used beer bottles has been emphasized in their re-use is in contrast with the stress on the physical function of the water bottle cloche, and this may reflect the priority on the aesthetic contemplation of nature in flower gardens as opposed to its exploitation in vegetable gardens. While these two sets of values can coexist and have strong relationships – the same person can be a vegetable grower and enjoy creating a garden for contemplation and get some of the same satisfaction from both – they are nonetheless different in their implications for the standards and values that are relevant in the two practices. The standards that guide people's actions in the practice of flower gardening would make it feel inappropriate to have an object with an obvious label exposed and redundant features, such as the handle on the top of the plastic water bottle. One side-effect of re-using the bottles as path edging is to almost completely disguise them – they no longer 'read' as bottles but seem more like shiny pebbles set in the ground; their material is emphasized and its elemental qualities fit the setting. Keeping in mind the discussion of materials in Chapter 2, the differences between the materials perhaps most keenly indicate the difference between what feels appropriate in the two settings; the understanding of glass as more 'natural' and plastic as more 'technical' lines up with the locations in which the two types of packaging have been re-used.

Moving inside the house, there follow some examples of packaging re-use in interior spaces – living areas as well as the bathroom and kitchen. The examples of packaging re-use in Figures 3.3, 3.4 and 3.5 below are similar to the cloche example in that they are serving a clear physical function. But this has required little inventiveness, because they continue to serve the purpose they were designed for – as containers. Re-using a pack in this way may seem unremarkable, but while unspectacular and not part of a public performance of self through objects, it indicates a basic and largely hidden level of re-use that serves only a utilitarian purpose. However, even these examples still have a relationship to the ideas discussed above about what might motivate people to re-use packaging. In their straightforward relationship to function they reflect Hendrick's 'instinct to master' referred to above, as well as having a likely relationship to values of thrift. These are relatively uncomplicated motivations which are tied up with ordering and caring for our immediate environment, performances of self to some degree, though without an obvious audience because they are generally not on display.

This function of re-used packaging in helping us to order our surroundings as we care for them is only possible in this case because the containers remain intact after their primary use – to perform in this way packaging has to remains 'useful', full of potential further uses. However, the authors' research has identified some features of such containers that serve as barriers to their re-use,

Figure 3.3 Metal packaging used to store garden supplies

Source: Authors

Figure 3.4 Cardboard packaging used to store garden seeds

Source: Authors

Figure 3.5 Plastic ice-cream box used to store bird food

Source: Authors

and which relate to the discussion here because they play on the cultural expectations that we bring to them. The appearance of containers after they have served their primary purpose has a marked effect on people's readiness to re-use them. A simple glass jar with a screw lid is, broadly speaking, more likely to be re-used if it fits expectations of acceptable appearance. These expectations seem to require that the jar is distinctive, in other words that it has an interesting form, but that it does not carry obvious signs of its initial use, in other words it is symbolically 'neutral' and carries no branding, like the jars in Figure 3.6 that have been filled with various spices and ingredients displayed in a kitchen. The jar in Figure 3.7, which has been re-used to hold cotton buds, satisfies the same criteria, suggesting that the same standards apply in the bathroom.

It seems to be the relatively neutral appearance of these jars that is important for their re-use, as it makes it possible for their owners to put them to work in a domestic scheme that carries their own imprint, not the brand the jars carried in their primary use – they afford an opportunity for the performance of self. If these jars had been made with labels that could not be removed, they may not have been so readily re-used. The authors' research suggests that this barrier to re-use exists with plastic containers too, even though they may be used less often than glass vessels in the public presentation of self. Individuals expressed less willingness to re-use containers where the label and graphics could not be removed. One participant made this remark about the plastic container in Figure 3.8, which is strong enough to serve another function but which has the graphics printed onto the plastic of the container itself.[7]

There is a sense here that if they are to be re-used, some types of packaging need to make it easy to fit into an individual's taste patterns by being more symbolically neutral than when they served their function as

Figure 3.6 Glass jars re-used in the kitchen

Source: Authors

Figure 3.7 Glass jar re-used in the bathroom
Source: Authors

packaging. This principle seems to apply to the examples just introduced, which involve clear physical function which in varying degrees is combined with the potential to indicate their owner's taste. This physical function is not necessarily present in the examples of re-use that follow. Here the aspects of people's relationship to re-use that are in play seem to rely more clearly on taste judgements. These packaging objects continue to serve a purpose in their re-use; they continue to fulfil a type of function, but this is based solely on their owners' liking for the way they look and their desire to display them – this is socio not techno-function. The blue glass bottles in Figure 3.9, displayed in a living area to catch the light in an ensemble with candles which emphasizes the play of light over and through the glass, exemplify this.

Figure 3.8 Mozzarella container

Source: Authors

Different taste judgements are relevant in the different spaces of the home, which are different fields of judgement in Bourdieu's terms.[8] Showing good taste in each space, being able to distinguish between what goes and what clashes, involves different criteria and requires different knowledge. In the example in Figure 3.9, it seems to be the deep blueness of the blue glass along with the carefully detailed simplicity of its form that makes what is just a blue glass bottle desirable beyond its initial function. Being displayed gives it a 'system function' – to demonstrate something about the taste of its owner in the symbolic system that is the interior scheme.

For some people, the desire to display packaging objects coincides with a desire to collect one type of object or another – including branded products. The tendency to collect things is a subject in itself and one that repays attention as a type of consumption that always has a certain intensity and occasionally has pathological dimensions. Collecting has an opposite character to consumption in general, when the word is understood in the sense of using things up, and has added resonance when the objects collected are packaging, which is designed with no function other than to be used up on the way to the goods it protects. This may be what makes packaging a particularly collectable type of artefact, since the desire to collect things as a way of preserving, ordering and saving them may be more keenly felt the more ephemeral the thing collected – such as the 'dolls, comic books, beer cans and match books' itemised by Russell Belk (2006). Belk defines collecting in this way:

The process of actively, selectively and passionately acquiring and possessing things removed from ordinary use and perceived as part of a set of non-identical objects or experiences.   *(Belk, 1995, p67)*

Figure 3.9 Glass
bottles on display
Source: Authors

The collection of Coca Cola bottles in Figure 3.10, found in the process of the authors' research, is a good example of the activities that Belk considers. It is a small but clearly valued collection and, as Belk (1995) and others, including Sigmund Freud, have noted, it is likely to play a significant role in the self-identity of its owner. The collection is displayed with the brand names clearly visible, suggesting that its display follows a different set of rules than that seen in the glass bottles and jars just discussed. The prominence of the graphics in the collection suggests that there is a strong positive relationship between the brandedness of the bottles and the collector's feelings towards them – the collector has 'bought' the brand in a distinctive and possibly more powerful way than is the case in conventional consumption; the collection is a celebration of the brand progressing through time, marked by the changing form of the bottles giving an authentic connection to part of history.

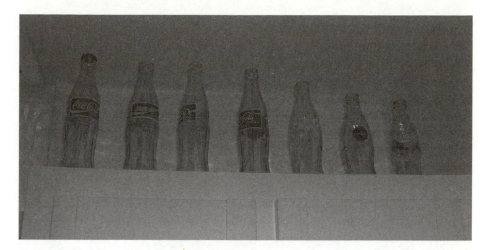

Figure 3.10 Collection of Coca Cola bottles

Source: Authors

The same individual made the collection of objects displayed in a cabinet shown in Figure 3.11. This is a different type of collection – it does not fit Belk's criteria for collecting, as it is made up of disparate objects, some of which are items of packaging that its owner has brought back from trips abroad. This example seems to fit better with what Michael Schiffer (1981) calls a 'conservatory' practice of re-use. The collection of objects seems to serve their owner as an aide memoir of his trips; they are accompanied by folders of documentation relating to the places he has visited. But like his collection of Coca Cola bottles, the display of this set of objects, grouped in their special glazed cabinet in his living room, seems to be significant for his sense of himself, perhaps to present himself as a discerning traveller as well as to allow him to reflect on the experiences he had while abroad. So in this group of objects packaging is re-used as a focus for rumination, an example perhaps of what Pierre Nora (1989) has called '*lieux de memoire*' – a place for memories that is part of what Jennifer Gonzales (1995) has called an 'autotopography', a making of the self through domestic spaces and objects.

Conclusion

It is difficult to maintain the separation of one aspect of re-use from another – the material, the human, the spatial – as will have been evident from the discussion above. The re-use examples introduced highlighted the relationship of people's dispositions to re-use packaging or not to their ideas about

Figure 3.11 Collection of objects, including packaging, from overseas trips

Source: Authors

the environment and to the practices of consumption of which packaging is part. They highlight the influence on reuse of feelings about what are appropriate actions and performances of self-identity, showing that feelings, as much as reason, are important. Each example involves specific materials and takes place in specific parts of the domestic environment – these elements work together every time packaging is re-used.

The re-use examples demonstrate some of the aspects of people that are relevant to re-use in action – they are qualities of thrift, environmental concern, inventiveness and a desire to control one's surroundings in action. They underline the fact that people do overcome the 'functional fixedness' which the objects we encounter present to us. This suggests that this fixedness is balanced to some extent by people seeing opportunities and 'openings' in familiar objects, seeing beyond the conventional life-story of packaging. Some designs, those 'open' designs which have built into them potential affordances for further uses, may facilitate working against this fixedness.

The relationship of self-identity to re-use seems to work differently when packaging is re-used for its physical function than when it is re-used for the purposes of display, and this has some implications for the physical form of packaging that is defined by design. As well as the exercise of creativity, the former involves the imposition of personality on an object that must first be rendered neutral and blank in appearance. The latter seems to draw only on the symbolic register of objects, to activate only their visual properties or their provenance. When displayed simply for what they are, without modification, pieces of packaging exist as part of a series of production that is engaged with through conventional consumption, rather than through the more or less radical reinvention that characterizes re-use for physical function.

This suggests that design interventions, which are the subject of Chapter 5, might respond differently to these two types of re-use, designing into packaging different sets of potential affordances. Packaging that can have a second life fulfilling a physical function might do this best if it is a relatively 'open' type of object that can easily be rendered neutral and stripped of its commercial identity – open for the identity of its re-user to be applied to it. Packaging designed to be re-used for its symbolic properties would need to fit readily into taste formations already in existence. Before getting specific about how these two principles might play out in practice, we will review in detail the spaces in which re-use takes place.

Notes

1   See www.defra.gov.uk/Environment/business/scp/.
2   Here, 'used' usually means literally that, something that has been used, rather than 'second hand'. It is safe to assume that the person re-using packaging is usually part of the same family as the person who bought the pack in the first place, if not that person themselves.
3   For studies of user innovation see Urban and Von Hippel, 1988; Shaw, 1993 and 1998; Franke and Shah, 2003; Luthje, Herstatt and Von Hippel, 2005.
4   Von Hippel uses the economic concept of 'rent' to explain the motivation for conventional innovation. The economic drivers that produce a desire/need for innovation may never apply to packaging re-use – the cheapest route for packaging in terms of effort and money expended has historically been straight into the bin, though this may change if the costs to consumers of waste disposal increase.
5   Andreas Reckwitz (2002, p253) suggests that knowledge in a practice 'embraces ways of understanding, knowing how, ways of wanting and of feeling that are linked to each other'.
6   Deborah Lupton (1998) offers a very useful overview of theories of emotion, noting a spectrum of theories between views of emotions as 'biologic' and 'constructed' – the former reducing them to their physical aspects, the latter concentrating on the ways in which they are constructed by culture.
7   The design of the graphics – leaving the plastic plain at either end of the tub – makes it appear as if they are printed on a separable label. The participant reported being fooled to the extent that they spent some time trying to remove the non-existent label. A consumer for whom re-usable packaging is a desirable feature of a pack might be encouraged to buy this product on false pretences.
8   In his study of taste, the sociologist Pierre Bourdieu suggested that:

> There are as many fields of preferences as there are fields of stylistic possibilities. Each of these worlds ... provides the small number of distinctive features which, functioning as a system of differences, differential deviations, allow the most fundamental social differences to be expressed almost as completely as through the most complex and refined expressive systems available in the legitimate arts; and it can be seen that the total field of these fields offers well-nigh inexhaustible possibilities for the pursuit of distinction.   (Bourdieu, 1984, p227)

4

Spaces, Habits
and Routines

Introduction

As packaging makes its way through our homes, whether it is re-used or not can depend on its material qualities and on the dispositions of its temporary owners. The previous two chapters have discussed the material and human qualities that seem to be relevant to this but have not emphasized their location in time and space – the where and when of packaging re-use. This chapter focuses on the ways that the physical arrangement of our domestic spaces influence packaging re-use and some of the ways that their built form both reflects the assumption that everyday life produces packaging waste and affords opportunities to divert some of it for a second life fulfilling a secondary function.

Our domestic spaces contain domestic routines and in some ways determine them. We follow these routines without necessarily considering them very carefully – they are what social theorists call our everyday 'practices'. The domestic spaces where we carry them out affect and determine them through the assumptions they bring with them, as well as through their physical arrangement. It is one of the premises of this book that there are moments in everyday life when the usually short life-span of packaging is extended by re-use that in some way breaks with these routines, these normal practices. Such a break may be the consequence of some potential that shows itself in a person's commitment to particular objects that form part of their performance of self. As Chapter 3 showed, these performances may draw on a disposition to thrift, or demonstrate inventiveness by finding a secondary function for packaging, or demonstrate good taste by simply displaying it.

This chapter discusses all the spaces of the home, exterior ones as well as interior ones. As the examples discussed in Chapter 3 demonstrated, packaging is re-used in all sorts of living areas, including gardens, and different taste rules govern what is acceptable in each type of space. Living rooms, kitchens, bathrooms, gardens and allotments are all sites of packaging re-use, but different factors influence it in each type of space. Among the most important of these spaces for re-use are those that are out of sight, where the rules of taste do not apply. Our research has shown that these spaces – the 'twilight zones' of our homes – can be significant staging posts in the progress of packaging from carrier bag to waste bin and can be spaces where packaging objects can acquire a new function through being taken out of the normal flow. These are the spaces in cupboards, sheds, bureaux, lofts, on the tops of wardrobes, where things that are too good to throw away linger for a while, perhaps to eventually be married up with a secondary use.

To the extent that the normal flow of packaging through the home requires that packaging become waste as soon as its primary function is finished, these spaces are subversive because they disrupt this flow. They are also subversive as they cut across the assumption inherited from 20th century modernism that many of these spaces – kitchens and bathrooms especially – will be efficient in their processing of waste material. This assumption grows out of and reinforces the 20th century recasting of homes as factories in reverse, units whose product is waste generated from processing the commodities that enter the home. Packaging waste is a very noticeable, and sometimes inconvenient, product of this domestic processing, this productive consumption, but only once it has reached the bin; keeping packaging for a possible rainy day when it may become useful cuts across the morality of hygiene and elimination around which many of our domestic spaces are now designed.

The chapter starts by considering the space of the kitchen – where a good proportion of packaging is processed and which is therefore usually the location of the bin which is its route out of the house. The degree to which the design of kitchens determines what happens in them is considered in the context of the idea of the history of kitchen design. Attention then turns to the spaces in which packaging can lurk after its first use, either out of sight, waiting perhaps for a further physical function, or on display as part of the interior décor of the home. Two types of twilight zone are identified: one that holds items for a potential further physical use – for a rainy day – and another that holds items that have an aesthetic function, either as part of their owner's private biography, and therefore often hidden, or as part of their public face in which case they are sometimes on display.

The movement of material in and out of these twilight zones is considered in the context of research on how people store and get rid of possessions. Some of the motivation for constructing and maintaining twilight zones comes from standards of tidiness and a widely held distaste for 'clutter'. This is discussed in the context of the productive ethic that influences the design of kitchens, and other domestic spaces, as well as a set of ideas about a tidy home reflecting a tidy (and therefore healthy) mind. Keeping packaging, even tidily, in principle subverts its usual flow to the bin and therefore contradicts aspects of this tidiness ethic. The reasons people keep items of packaging hidden away are therefore considered next and are shown to have a strong relationship to the aspect of self-identity that is closely associated with possessions – the 'extended self' in possessions that Russell Belk identifies (Belk, 1988).

It is characteristic of twilight zones that items circulate through them, and an example of this is considered in detail – a tin box for OXO cubes designed to be re-used. This object has acquired a new set of meanings in the current phase of its biography, partly due to cultural shifts that put particular value on the past and an increase in the desirability of objects that would once have been considered not to be in good taste. The relationship of kitsch to the flows of packaging into and through twilight zones is then considered, involving a discussion of the concept of kitsch itself and its re-interpretation as part of acceptable taste, influencing the emergence of old packaging as a 'collectable' item.

The chapter ends by going outside the home and considering how allotments, domestic gardens, sheds and garages come into play in arresting the flow of packaging to waste. Different sets of expectations apply in these spaces, apparently governed by how physically close they are to living spaces. So a use of packaging that is permissible and visible on an allotment would be inappropriate in a garden attached to a house, though it might be acceptable if it were hidden away in a shed or garage. The overlapping sets of constraints on what is acceptable in what parts of the domestic environment have some consequences that facilitate packaging re-use in particular places. One of these is that because these outside spaces are zones of relative freedom from constraint, they are places where it is easier to exercise the sort of self-reliant creativity on which re-use often depends.

The Idea of the Kitchen as a Factory

Ellen Lupton and Abott Miller (1992) describe the development in America of the domestic spaces that are involved in the processing of wastes of all sorts – both human waste and the waste from consumption. Their discussion of the latter traces the development of kitchen design and draws on the literature on domestic management that appeared between the late 19th and the mid 20th century, as well as on their own analysis of the design of kitchens and the new types of furniture that were developed for them. A significant element in the historical background to their discussion of the idea of the 'continuous kitchen' is Christine Frederick's 1919 application of F. W. Taylor's Scientific Management to the arrangement of kitchens. They note that the influence of Taylorism on the modernization of the design of kitchens coincided with the increased prevalence of packaged foods (Lupton and Miller, 1992, pp41ff) as part of the development of modern consumerism. This acceptance of waste in the processing of household provisions through the domestic space led, among other things, to the kitchen bin becoming a standard part of the necessary equipment.

Lupton and Miller's work is a useful starting point for thinking about how our domestic arrangements affect packaging re-use, but it is limited to describing the factors that influenced the development of kitchen and bathroom arrangements in middle-class homes in the 20th century and the 'genealogy' of the arrangements of furniture and architecture that resulted. It also implies that design and theories of hygiene and domestic management to a significant extent determine what goes on in these domestic spaces. In other words, their line of reasoning seems to assume that what people do in their kitchens is determined by their design, in which the values of hygiene and 'civilization' are embedded. While they do describe some designs for kitchens that responded to late 20th century concerns with sustainability – for instance integrating dedicated spaces for composting into a kitchen design – their account is mainly motivated by an interest in past influences on domestic arrangements, rather than in contemporary forces that may change these arrangements.

Their discussion of the factory analogy emphasizes how the rational values of the modernized workplace that began to be built into domestic spaces loaded a variety of (unfulfilling) responsibilities onto the middle-class house-wife. As they put it:

> The modern home moulds consumerist bodies, trained to embrace the logic of the consumer economy and its cycle of ingestion and waste. (Lupton and Miller, 1992, p11)

There seems to be an assumption here that the design of spaces, furniture, appliances and products wholly determines the actions of the domestic worker, 'disciplined' by their surroundings and the regimes embedded in them. Lupton and Miller refer here to the work of Michel Foucault, citing his *Discipline and Punish*, in which he lays out the ways in which human subjects are 'docile' bodies locked into regimes of power (Foucault, 1977). While our physical surroundings clearly do influence how we 'work' – whether in employ-ment or at home, in commercial factories or domestic ones – and we do inter-nalize the 'regimes of truth' that are built into them, given that this book is about people *breaking* such rules by re-using packaging, it is important to look beyond Lupton and Miller's assumptions about the power of our environ-ment to influence our actions.

The reading of Foucault to which Lupton and Miller seem to subscribe – that individuals are passive and do not act outside the pervasive and domi-nating regime of power – is not the only one available. For instance, a critique of such a reading from the field of education (Butin, 2001) notes that in his own later work Foucault allowed that our relationship to regimes of power necessarily involves the 'possibility of resistance'. The concern of this book is to identify the moments when people get round the edge of the regimes that are built into the hardware of everyday life. Waste is designed into packaging and the system of provisioning that requires it; re-use is the subversion of this regime of waste – resistance to it. The examples in this book demonstrate the fact that people do spontaneously re-use packaging and that they do this *despite* the 'disciplinary regime' built into both packaging and the places in which people use it – shops, kitchens, living rooms. It is clear that even within a highly 'disciplinary' set of arrangements for provisioning and transporting goods, scope exists for relatively free movement – creativity even.

This creativity is the ability to see in a piece of packaging usefulness that is outside that function built into it by its 'proper' place in the design–production–consumption circuit. It is possible to understand our usual *inability* to see such potential functions in Foucauldian terms, and this may help us to understand something more about how the design of packaging can work against the 'regime' and promote the ability to see and create openings for re-use. The fact that we continually monitor the degree to which we conform to 'proper' behaviour – what Foucault calls surveillance – perhaps explains our habitual inability to see opportunities for re-use in packaging. The possibility of resistance is always present; the potential always exists for us to find alternatives to the flow of packaging from commodity to waste through personalized variations in the routines on which that flow depends, but although doing so is common, it is not the norm.

A disruption in our routine way of dealing with packaging seems to be necessary to our seeing in it some potential for re-use. That disruption can result from a change in our thinking – an increased awareness of the implications that our habits have for environmental sustainability is one such – or a new need not encountered before. Being a parent, for instance, introduces a set of physical needs that do not feature in the lives of the childless, some of which can be met by re-using packaging. For all that Lupton and Miller take a somewhat deterministic approach to the relationship between domestic design and individuals' behaviour, they do recognize that changes in people's concerns can lead them to engage with their material surroundings as active agents rather than passive disciplined bodies. They note, for instance, that people adapt their kitchen furniture to accommodate recycling and composting, writing of 'innovative consumers struggling to fashion answers out of the inadequate pool of equipment available for recycling in the home' (1992, p72).

The authors' research has shown that the domestic innovation of new functions for packaging has particular relationships to the spaces of the home and follows certain rhythms: packaging arrives in the home and may spend a long time between first use and disposal, waiting for a secondary use in a 'twilight zone'. These spaces appear in the kitchen as well as living areas, bedrooms, outbuildings and gardens. The next section describes these and their role in packaging re-use, tracing the ways that the progress of packing from carrier bag to bin may be delayed by re-use.

The Twilight Zone – A 'Between' Space

The kitchen cupboard – the one the kitchen designer fitted in to fill up the space, but which is not actually very useful – the wardrobe drawer in the spare bedroom, the shed, the shelf in the cellar, the attic 'box room' – all these can be twilight zones for packaging that interrupt its normal processing as waste. There is nothing very remarkable, perhaps, in stashing a piece of packaging away for a rainy day, and the dispositions towards objects discussed in Chapter 3 are likely to influence who does this and why, but in the context of the very large quantities of packaging waste that flow through our homes, the spontaneous use of parts of the home to disrupt this flow deserves attention. Gregson et al (2007a and b) describe how people get rid of other types of unwanted item, but do not deal with packaging in their discussion of the flows of objects through the home. This justifies considering packaging in this way here. Like the types of used commodity that Gregson et al concentrate on, packaging objects also sometimes pause in their trajectory to the waste stream. Such pauses contradict the common assumption about the sustainability of our consumption practices, an assumption that characterises them as a problematic part of a 'throw-away' society. The persistence of packaging in certain spaces of the home demonstrates that we do not have exclusively short-term relationships with it but sometimes invest it with meanings that contradict its designed-in status as waste. These meanings reflect our sense of our selves and our concerns about the effect of our consumption on our environment.

Twilight zones for packaging may be an example of the 'temporary resting points' for possessions that Gregson et al (2007a, p8) refer to in their research into the diverse ways in which possessions make their way from attachment to 'ridding'. A common feature of twilight zones is that they are out of sight; they allow packaging to gently acquire a new function, exempted from the tidiness and order that usually create the incentive to move packaging swiftly into the bin – they are spaces at the edge of normal practice in the home, out of sight but potentially still in mind. These spaces are where people save things for a rainy day, recognizing their potential value but keeping them in the twilight of a space that is hidden from view.

Chapter 3 described another type of collection of packaging that is arrested in its journey to the waste stream to be kept and displayed in living areas. These collections are different from 'rainy day' twilight zones, because here the things collected have acquired their secondary use. Whereas packaging saved for a rainy day waits to be re-activated by some creative intervention, the display of Coca Cola bottles in Figure 3.10 is serving its purpose in a collection. The collection of 'interesting' packaging, the strangely shaped bottles of undrinkable liqueur of lurid colours that sit on the sideboard to show your friends you can afford frequently to go abroad on holiday, is doing its new thing (Figure 4.1). These objects have found their new purpose and are already being re-used, though this is aesthetic as opposed to instrumental re-use.

Nonetheless, such 'shrines' are also clearly identifiable areas of domestic space that disrupt the passage of packaging from carrier bag to bin, so in a sense they are twilight zones too, even though they are not out of sight. Although the packaging in them is not out of sight and may in the case of the Coca Cola bottles have acquired economic as well as personal value, it is in principle only arrested in its progress to the bin. The feelings evoked by collecting identified by Belk (1995), where objects are actively selected and removed from ordinary use, providing memories of the past and the sense of satisfaction in a completed collection of similar objects, may be at work in shrine twilight zones. As Michael Thompson (1979) showed, objects lose and acquire value, so packaging displayed in a shrine can always rejoin the conventional flow and revert to being waste.

In terms of Goffman's categories for 'front-stage' and 'back-stage' aspects of everyday performances, these two types of twilight zone are respectively back-stage (rainy day) and front-stage (shrines). The authors' research uncovered some variety in both types of twilight zone for packaging, which indicates the creative element in packaging re-use. The consignment of packaging to twilight zones is integrated into related everyday practices, so the thrifty practice of saving things for a rainy day in some cases itself requires re-using packaging – the cardboard box in which items are kept is itself re-used in the process. The types of spaces in which packaging can linger include zones in the house such as garden sheds, garages and cellars; dedicated storage such as food cupboards, drinks cabinets, wardrobes and medicine cabinets; and portable spaces such as shoe-cleaning kits and sewing boxes. Most of these are spaces that are out of sight, which suggests that most twilight zones contain packaging waiting for that opportunity for it to be re-used and that packaging shrines may be less common.

The physical properties of packaging are relevant to whether it ends up in a twilight zone. The physical properties of some types of packaging mean it is simply not useful for anything after it has served its initial purpose. The film that wraps food and other goods has so little integrity that it ceases to *be* an object once the pack is opened and becomes instead an awkward material that is often contaminated with whatever it has contained and simply presents a problem for disposal. It may also stimulate feelings of frustration, given the amount of waste plastic film and carton board that households generate and the patchy coverage of facilities to recycle it.

Because it loses its physical integrity once it has finished serving the purpose it was designed for, there is no obvious way this type of packaging

Figure 4.1 Liqueur bottle collection

Source: Authors

Figure 4.2 Carrier bag twilight zone

Source: Authors

could be re-used. The fact that packaging made of film ceases to have a clear shape when it has been used makes it more akin to a material that could be made into something else than an object for which an alternative use could be found. If sorting facilities exist, it can be recycled – rendered into a new, lower grade, material from which new products can be made – but to re-use/re-make it in the domestic environment would require a domestic 'system' that functioned rather differently to those that usually provide secondary functions for packaging. There are no obvious uses for this type of material in itself in the domestic environment other than as material from which to make something. This characteristic makes plastic film an interesting case when thinking how to promote packaging re-use through design, because the physical incoherence that makes plastic film impossible to re-use in itself, and therefore unlikely to be collected in a twilight zone, reinforces the fact that physical coherence is a necessary characteristic of packaging that can be re-used.

Twilight zones, then, are spaces that interrupt the flow of packaging to the waste stream, holding types of object that retain enough physical coherence to allow them to be re-used in their existing form, or with a little modification. These places where packaging is saved for a further physical use are usually out of sight, but are related in principle to collections of packaging that are often deliberately put on display, because both contain objects arrested in their flow to the waste stream. On arriving in such a 'shrine', packaging is immediately fulfilling a function as part of a collection put together for its role in curating the narrative of its owner's life with objects.

In and Out of the Twilight Zone

There are likely to be a variety of reasons why packaging enters a twilight zone that derive from the various relationships between packaging in a twilight zone and its owner. Reasons for consigning packaging to a twilight zone seem to range from a conscious desire to be thrifty and to minimize waste to the inertia that can overtake possessions that for no clear reason are not got rid of but are stored. Putting packaging into a twilight zone because of a desire to be thrifty involves at least an intention to find a secondary use for the stored packaging and sometimes a clear plan for its secondary use. However, the relationships to objects in the latter case are more difficult to determine, because they are likely to be to do with their owner's biography and the associations that are tied up with the objects.

Thinking of consumption at the scale of a social phenomenon, such relationships are acknowledged to be unstable – they change over time and as objects circulate through different spaces:

All commodities have social, technical, cultural and economic biographies, they mean different things to different people at different times and in different places, classified and reclassified into endlessly reconstructed cultural categories. (Kopytoff, 1986, p68)

Kopytoff was referring to the biography of commodities at the scale of the economy and culture at large rather than as private possessions, but they are no less affected by classification and reclassification while they are in this phase of our lives. Gregson et al (2007a) identify family relationships – relationships of care and love closely related to individual identity – as powerful influences on the re-evaluation and the reclassification of possessions and their re-distribution, to family, friends or to the waste stream. Although packaging was excluded from their study, varieties of classification and reclassification are evident at the moments when packaging enters and leaves a twilight zone. Criteria for this classification are evident around decisions to consign packaging to, or retrieve it from, a twilight zone, and some of these criteria, because they rely on properties of the packaging itself, can in principle be designed into it.

A good deal of the decision-making about whether to keep a piece of packaging for re-use is based in practicality – to make it into a twilight zone a piece of packaging has to be more or less physically 'coherent', in other words it has to have enough strength and structure to be a candidate for a second life. It has to be capable of some further use, whether or not that use is clear at the moment it is diverted from the waste. Very often, however, an object's potential further use *is* evident to the person putting the object in the twilight zone: they have a plan for its future. So a collection of yoghurt pots in a drawer, a box of tin cans on a shelf in the shed, a selection of glass jars in a kitchen cupboard saved from recycling may all have an intended purpose.[1]

Beyond having the coherence to withstand a further use that makes them qualify for being saved for the future, there are other physical aspects of pack designs that may affect how easy they are to store and therefore may encourage them to be saved. The yoghurt pots in Figure 4.3 nest deeply one inside the other and therefore do not take up a great deal of space, while other types of packaging may not be so convenient to keep. The more awkwardly shaped they are, the more difficult it is to create a twilight zone for them that fits easily into conventional kitchen arrangements and the workflow of the domestic 'factory'. For this reason, perhaps, twilight zones for packaging are often found in more marginal spaces such as sheds, garages and cellars, with fewer constraints on space (Figure 4.4).

Figure 4.3 Yoghurt pot twilight zone

Source: Authors

Figure 4.4 Interior of shed

Source: Authors

Packaging is consigned to or removed from twilight zones through processes of classification and re-classification. In these processes the material qualities and human dispositions that were the subject of discussion in the previous two chapters come into play in combination with particular zones in the domestic environment – in marginal spaces that conceal the saved packaging out of sight, and possibly out of mind, for some future purpose; in public spaces where packaging forms props for the front-stage performance of self-identity; or in hidden spaces for items that have a more private relationship to the self. Packaging in all of these spaces remains part of the flow of commodities through the home, and the criteria that determine when it is consigned to or removed from these spaces relate closely to those that affect other types of object. So the fact that packaging is assumed to require its 'place', and that it should not be 'out of place', to use Mary Douglas's (1966) classic definition for dirt, derives from the cultural patterns that govern household management as a whole. Powerful among these is the set of expectations around tidiness and efficiency which appears in recent discourse as a set of views on 'clutter' in the home – an ethic that relates tidiness and organization to personal worth. It is in the nature of packaging to clutter, it being the excess left over from the process of acquisition, and, apart from the bin, twilight zones are the only alternative available to manage this excess through the spaces of the home.

Twilight Zones and 'Clutter'

The packaging saved for a rainy day in a twilight zone may have a potential further physical use, but this potential may never be fulfilled. If so, from a certain point of view, the objects in such a twilight zone, instead of resting between two states, may have more in common with a hoard, a collection of objects with no obvious future purpose, kept only for the sake of keeping them. Such a collection is no longer part of an apparently purposeful system with a new 'system function' as its end point. The apparent lack of purpose in such a collection breaks the rules of efficiency that govern many aspects of the design of our homes and the norms of behaviour that affect our actions in them. The power of these norms, and their limits, was evident in the authors' research when individuals exhibited embarrassment when showing stored packaging items for which they had no clear future plan, describing them-selves negatively by using the word 'hoarder'.

The productive ethic that Lupton and Miller identified built into the kitchen-as-factory also extends to other parts of our domestic spaces. There is an expectation that our relationship to living areas and areas devoted to storage should also be based on order and productivity. However, in these other spaces this relationship is assumed to mirror not so much the order and productivity of the factory as the supposed order of a healthy mind. In recent years this aspect of our relationship to our domestic surroundings has been evident in the promotion of a relationship between tidiness – domestic order and efficient domestic management – and a morally and psychologically 'good' life that is healthy, independent, purposeful, productive and forward-looking. Clutter is taken to be the antithesis of this ethic.

This ethic is evident in the media and in popular psychology literature on how to organize our homes, to get rid of 'clutter', to remove unnecessary possessions and thereby obtain peace of mind. This was the idea behind a 2002 BBC TV series called *Life-Laundry* and associated books (the presenter of the BBC programme, Dawna Walter, published two books of the same name).[2] Walter implies that hoarding is an inherently bad thing to do and that our living spaces need to be regularly cleansed of unused possessions, regularly purged of the matter out of place that will pollute our homes, and by extension our minds. Along with this idea comes the implication that to be good consumers we must get rid of possessions that we are not using. Sociologists Saulo Cwerner and Alan Metcalfe discuss the relationship between this de-cluttering ethic and storage (2003) and note that the question of what constitutes clutter, whether it is in fact a negative aspect of domestic arrangements and how it relates to the storage of objects in the home is under-researched. They suggest that rather than being a necessarily bad thing, clutter is a symptom of what they identify as a complex layering of time and space in the home as objects circulate through it.[3]

Studies of how people relate to the possessions they store contradict the assumption that psychological health depends on a regular cleansing or purging of the home of unused items. The authors' research demonstrates that even items as relatively ephemeral as packaging are sometimes kept for long periods, and sometimes with no clear sense that they will have a further use, but only in case they do, or because they mean something to their owners. Woodward's ethnographic study of women's everyday clothing practices (2007) shows that what women keep in their wardrobes has a close relationship to their sense of themselves, and that although they may be 'gone through' to clear out unused items, this does not alter that fact or stop women keeping some clothes for a long time. The caches of used packaging that accumulate in people's houses seem to have the potential to be significant in equivalent ways.

For those people minded to do so, those with the appropriate disposition, the fact they have a collection of used packaging waiting for a new function seems not to have a damaging effect on their psyche, as the contemporary discourse of 'life-laundry' would have it, but rather to give them a sense of positively resisting the assumption of disposability built into packaging, a resistance that is positive for their sense of self as it serves an environmentally concerned disposition to material goods. Their attachment to this packaging as a resource for re-use also fits with the observation that some researchers, such as Ruth Mugge (2008 and 2007), have made that as consumers we are more attached to things we have customized, or which we have had a hand in designing. Re-used packaging fits both categories, and the attachment to it that is a consequence of someone having re-used it, or even having kept it with the intention to re-use it, seems to quite clearly contradict the ethic of the life-laundry.

So if clutter is not necessarily bad and people do keep some packaging despite its inherent disposability, it is worth considering why.

The Hidden Shrine – Re-use Potential that is Beyond Design

The differences between storing packaging for a future physical use and keeping a collection of packaging on display as part of the narration of identity seem quite clear, but the distinction between these two types of twilight zone are somewhat confounded by instances where people keep packaging with no likely future physical function tucked away in a hidden space. These hidden shrines seem to contain items that are kept simply because their owner likes them or because they have a strong relationship to their sense of self. That relationship may be based on the fact that the packaging that has been kept is particularly tasteful or fashionable, drawing on shared values in other words, or the relationship may be more quirky, based on personal experiences that result in feelings of attachment to the objects. This type of relationship between the object and its owner's biography gives such collections particular potency in respect of the owner's sense of self.

Some recent work that has considered how to use design to encourage longer-term attachment to products – against the ethic of the 'throw-away society' – seems to downplay the role of this personalized and relatively arbitrary aspect of attachment to objects. Chapman (2005), for instance, makes a good deal of the ways that the design of all sorts of products may encourage their owners to be attached to them for longer but does not remark on the ways in which mundane items have the potential to remain important to their owners over long periods, and, in the case of ephemera like packaging, despite their designers' intentions. The reason for this lack of concern may be because the specifics of the design of these objects have by definition little to do with their owner's attachment to them – they are designed not to last. From the perspective of design they are therefore uncomfortable examples of attachment, because the relationship between them and their owners is beyond the power of design to influence.

However, it is not in principle beyond the power of design to work with the fact that people do develop attachments to ephemeral things like packaging strong enough that they will keep them for quite long periods. Two examples of this sort from the authors' research involved women who had kept perfume packaging, a type of object with which women might be expected to develop an engaged relationship, and where the design and the brand are likely to be important to their feelings of attachment. Opening a wardrobe drawer where she had some items of packaging, one interviewee, 'Linda', a female in middle age, talked about the reasons she kept a pink perfume box:

Here it is – now that's a box I like, I've had that now for about two years. I think it had Marks and Spencer's perfume in it originally.

Asked what she had kept in it she replied:

Nothing – I've just kept the box because it is nice, I've kept it because I thought I might buy something and want a nice box.

Linda's mention of the brand name suggests that this may have influenced her decision to keep the box, but this is not what she draws attention to – she emphasizes that she has kept the box 'because it is nice', because it means something to her, though she does not say exactly what. Her following statement about a possible physical function for the box seems to have less weight, partly because it is not an especially clear plan for the box's future and partly because she seems to have added it to her rationalization as an afterthought.

Perfume packaging also features in the next example. 'Georgia', who is in her early twenties, described in detail a perfume bottle she had kept for three years. This bottle incorporates an unconventional gimmick – a 'snow shaker' built into the top in which there is a tiny figure of a glamorous woman in an evening dress. She described displaying the bottle for its ornamental qualities until it was used up, but then keeping it 'put away somewhere'. The fact that the perfume was a birthday present may explain her emotional connection to it, and as in the previous example she describes the packaging as 'nice', encompassing both its aesthetic qualities and its personal meaning for her.

It is possible to get some idea of what characterizes the hidden shrines that these objects occupy in their 'afterlife' from some comments that Georgia made about the other objects she keeps in a box with her used-up perfume bottle:

Quite a lot of photographs are in there that I haven't sorted out yet. Odds and ends – I went on a hen night last year and there are odds and ends from that hen night in there. Sorts of things that you're not necessarily going to use again, but they are sentimental things – probably a sentimental box.

These comments suggest that this collection has a role in Georgia's sense of her self – these are things she has feelings for and their innate value is not important. They are, however, important to her, and when she was asked if she might dispose of the perfume bottle, she suggested it would stay in its hidden 'shrine':

It just seems too nice, it's probably cause I know it's expensive as well – it's probably the most expensive perfume I've ever been bought, so I think that probably had something to do with it, but I just liked it so that will probably stay.

The feelings for this object as a point of attachment for her memories, a '*lieux de memoire*' (Nora, 1989; Gonzales, 1995) seem of a different class to the economic argument for its value that she also introduces. However, they are part of the same rationale, because she was given the perfume – its cost is a marker of its importance as a gift, not of her sacrifice to afford it.

Neither of these items, bottle or box, was meant to last, but both were kept, though neither with an obvious future physical function in mind. This is a sort of hoarding, along similar lines to keeping possessions in what Gregson et al (2007a) call 'liminal' or border spaces – twilight zones. There is no purposeful end in mind for objects kept in this way, which can be of all sorts – clothes, electrical equipment, cars, furniture, sports equipment. If the sequence of events that these other types of possessions follow applies also to packaging, then once they fulfil their role to 'narrate a previous life', as Gregson et al put it, their designed-in destiny as waste is likely to reassert itself and they may find their way to the waste stream.

This is not inevitable, however. The movement of such objects out of a hidden shrine may be to a higher value, collectively validated through an emerging market. There are plenty of examples of objects following this path, outlined by Thompson in 1979, and it seems to apply particularly to packaging of certain types, possibly including perfume packaging such as that just described. If this is how objects emerge from a hidden twilight zone, then this hoarding of objects may be the equivalent of the pupa in an insect's lifecycle – the ugly caterpillar/waste packaging becomes a beautiful butterfly/valued antique through its matter being reconfigured in a chrysalis/twilight zone. Well-known examples of such revaluations of packaging include the decorative tins described in Chapter 1, such as the OXO tin in Figure 1.4. It would be possible to reconstruct the history of an item like this, in the spirit of the 'imagined histories' that Gregson and Crewe suggest may go along with second-hand goods. In doing so we are in a situation similar to that which faces archaeologists – while we know or can deduce some of the steps in the object's biography, we have an equivalent lack of knowledge of the specific details. Archaeologists Gosden and Marshall note that thinking about an object's 'cultural biography' makes it possible 'to understand the way objects become invested with meaning through the social interactions they are caught up in' (Gosden and Marshall, 1999, p170).

Although the type of social interactions that involve such things as an OXO tin – or packaging in general – may have a different scope than those which usually interest archaeologists, they are in principle no less significant in terms of the material culture of which they are part. The meanings designed into the tin through its graphic treatment were clearly intended to serve the commercial purposes of the OXO Company. The popular modernism of the styling fit the concept of this early convenience food, an invention that made it possible to have all the 'goodness' of meat stock without the labour and effort involved in making the real thing. The tin was designed with a second use in mind – its graphics include the slogan 'this tin makes an ideal lunch box' – and it seems likely that some tins were used for this purpose, though their size, strength and durability meant they were useful for boxing up many other things as well. However, using the tin as a lunchbox served the company's purposes particularly well. The engaging, anthropomorphic graphic identity – established early in the 20th century – would be promoted particularly effectively by the tin's re-use as a lunchbox. So in our imagined history of this box, the initial re-user may have been a factory worker leaving home each weekday morning with sandwiches wrapped in greaseproof paper in his OXO tin, perhaps carried in a canvas holdall. This re-user is a factory or site worker, not someone with access to a works canteen; a manual worker not an office worker.

Assuming, then, that someone used our tin to take their lunch to work for some period of time, it may then have ceased to serve this purpose – its meaning might have changed, in the light of changes in our material culture.[3] Specifically, it is likely to have been the introduction of lightweight plastic containers that would have ousted the OXO tin as a preferred container for a portable lunch. If the connotations of OXO – food processed for convenience in reliable, hygienic factory conditions – represented the progressive modernity of the middle of the 20th century, in later decades similar connotations became attached to plastics, the quintessentially modern material of the late 20th century. At this point in its biography, it is conceivable that another way of re-using the OXO tin would have been found. The meaning of its material, and possibly its graphic identity, having changed in the face of changes in domestic material culture, it might have ceased to be an appropriate prop in the front-stage display of the identity of a 'competent worker'.

At this point, its meaning having changed, another use may have been found for our tin, perhaps to store small things in a back-stage setting – a shed, a cellar or an outhouse. Clearly this type of function is well within the physical capacity of this type of packaging, and the new identity of the object in its altered relationship, possibly with the same person, may have therefore emphasized the structural aspects of its design over its symbolic 'content'. The fact that it was an OXO tin may have become less important than the fact that it was simply a useful, durable container with a close fitting lid. Some time may then have passed. The late 20th century cultural shifts that have seen a concern with an authentic past and a more equivocal relationship with ideas of progress are likely to have brought about another shift in meaning for this OXO tin.

The tin was bought by one of the authors at a car boot sale in 2001, offered for sale as a piece of collectable memorabilia, its meaning reconfiguring itself in response to an interest in the 'imagined history' of such second-hand objects, very much in the spirit that Gregson outlines. The tin now communicates something of a mythic modernity, associated with comforting, but probably inaccurate, stereotyped images in which factory workers use a tin like this to carry their sandwich lunch to work wrapped in grease-proof paper.

Shrines, Authenticity and Kitsch

Despite their probable inaccuracy, such images have a sense of authenticity; they feel true. In response to the need to capitalize on all ways of producing the sort of positive feelings that may result in sales, a good deal of commercial and academic attention has been paid to how such feelings come about. Some commentators have analysed these feelings with the objective of increasing the likelihood that products will be taken as authentic. Virginia Postrel (2003), for instance, discussing the importance of the aesthetic aspect of consumers' relationships to products, outlines the features of a sense of authenticity that is attractive to consumers. This conception of authenticity in principle comprises a set of characteristics that could be associated with objects through design, and only a little reflection is needed to identify products of all types where such qualities are deployed as part of a strategy to attract consumers.[5]

Postrel suggests that such authenticity has three manifestations: as purity – the most true; as tradition – the most trusted; and as aura – the signs of history (Postrel, 2003, p111).[6] While she offers this as an abstract scheme, she acknowledges that authenticity has a very significant personal dimension which is not within the reach of design. This personal dimension of authenticity has a social basis which means that what people feel is authentic changes through time (p16). The OXO tin discussed above has authenticity of aura in that it shows its age and carries the physical traces of its biography, as well as something of the authenticity of purity, since it really is as old as it looks, but its meaning for its owner will always have a personal dimension as well, as we saw with the perfume packaging discussed above.

Though the personal dimension of authenticity is in principle beyond the reach of design, marketing and brand development efforts respond to the changing social conceptions of what is or is not authentic for groups of consumers who share particular configurations of cultural capital. The changing nature of these conceptions leads back to the subject of this chapter – packaging's transit through the spaces of the home and its pauses along the way. Changes in conceptions of authenticity are likely to be linked to changes in how innately ephemeral objects are valued. Changes in personal views of the meaning of a piece of packaging kept in a hidden twilight zone may lead to it finding its way to the waste stream when it is re-evaluated in the light of new personal circumstances such as a new relationship (Gregson et al, 2007a). In an equivalent move that has different consequences, changes in shared conceptions of authenticity can mean an object like the OXO tin emerges from its twilight zone into the light as a more valuable object.

Although highly decorated tins have been made since late in the 19th century, their meaning had changed somewhat by the end of the 20th century in some quite subtle and complex ways. Thinking of them in terms of ideas of authenticity helps unpack this change in meaning, particularly considering the fact that by the late 20th century tins were being produced that were made to look like designs of 50 years before. Figure 4.5 shows such a tin, discovered in the process of the authors' research, re-used for storage. The trade in items like this as 'collectables' is well established and does not seem to distinguish very clearly between tins that are old and ones that simply look old. The important thing seems to be how they look – how they evoke the aura of a more authentic past. Figure 4.6 shows a display of tins fixed to a beam in a pub ceiling, some of which are older, others more recent.

This display, in its context of an interior stripped to bare wood, seems to be using the tins to contribute what Postrel might identify as authenticity in their aura of age and patina. None of the surfaces in the interior are evenly finished or coloured; they conjure a sense of history. In this way, the interior, and the tins in it, relate to a configuration of taste which has a particular relationship to the past and how the meaning of these tins has changed.

Kitsch is a somewhat contested concept, the meaning of which has changed since it became used to describe objects that were 'debased' in terms of their cultural value in the mid 20th century. The critic Clement Greenberg is credited with one of the earliest uses of the word, discussing the relationship between the avant-garde art that he considered important, and kitsch. For Greenberg, kitsch is a product of modernity, a polluting force that

Figure 4.5 Reproduction Thorntons tin

Source: Authors

Figure 4.6 Display of tins in a pub

Source: Authors

flattens cultural distinctiveness – a 'mass product of Western industrialism' (1939, p38).[7] These sentiments echo those that the avant-gardists themselves expressed about tinned food, which were referred to in Chapter 1 (Carey, 1992). Decorative tins, packaging for biscuits or other goods, were from their inception identified with mass culture in this way. They were always decorative, emphasized and promoted the manufacturer's brand, and, with advances in printing technology, often carried a reproduction of a work of realist art printed on the lid, in many cases of a particularly sentimental type. Under Greenberg's definition, these were doubly kitsch objects – they used and reproduced debased images from 'academic' art and they were agents of the mass food culture of Western industrialism.

The late 20th century saw another version of the concept of kitsch become prominent as part of the sometimes ironic celebration of consumption. This reorientation has emphasized a parallel sense of kitsch, not as a word used by members of the cultural elite, accompanied by a ready sneer to decry the misapplication of elite culture by the masses, but to indicate a clever ironic attitude to the tastefulness of things which has appeared in all parts of culture, from everyday consumption to high art. This tendency of kitsch to 'lend itself to irony' that Calinescu (1987, p230) identifies in the work of the late 19th century poet Rimbaud and the Dadaists in the early 20th century has re-emerged.

Now it is cool to embrace 'kitsch' objects, to show that your individual taste can rise above the crude division between good and bad taste that the other sense of the word invokes. This sense of kitsch, this 'ironic kitsch', means that in a culture where taste no longer trickles down to the masses from the elite, but diffuses through culture like dye through milk, objects like decorative tins gain different meanings. In a culture where taste preferences are no longer determined by economic position but by lifestyle and identity, anything is potentially fashionable, and fashion is atomized into as many versions of good taste as there are communities.

The ironic kitsch phenomenon allows ephemera to be appreciated by the knowing as an element in their front-stage life, demonstrating their knowledge. Decorative tins can leave the back-stage and become 'collectables', for display in carefully marshalled ensembles of kitchen and living room décor.[8] It is of course possible to design kitsch, though designers are not generally trained to aspire to this, rather they are taught that their profession has a variety of higher purposes that derive from the lasting modernist configuration of design as a culturally progressive discipline. While modernist principles of efficiency and formal creativity fit perfectly well with the engineering aspect of packaging design – many packs involve sophisticated card engineering – the elements of consumer packaging that are designed for their visual appeal have a more problematic relationship to those principles. The production and structural design required to make a decorative tin like the ones just discussed may be sophisticated, if dated, but the 'design' – in other words what is printed or embossed on the steel surface – is likely to be determined only by popular taste, not by any principles of high design. It will therefore always be more or less self-consciously kitsch.

This discussion of the spaces where packaging circulates in the home between the front door and the bin shows that it may linger in one of several types of twilight zone. Packaging moves out of some of these zones into a further physical use – a problem arises which stored packaging can solve. Other types of twilight zone capture packaging to serve no further physical purpose but instead to contribute to its owner's sense of themselves as part of an 'autotopography' (Gonzales, 1995).

Exterior spaces – Garden, Garage and Shed

In a private garden you want everything to look perfect – in an allotment you're not bothered – it's quite funny.

Distinct patterns of convention govern what types of thing can be used and kept for what purpose and for how long in various parts of the dwelling. The places in which the flow of packaging to the bin is arrested inside the house seem usually to be hidden, whereas a rather more relaxed set of rules seems to govern spaces that are not part of the living area of the house where people also keep and re-use packaging. The rules of domestic propriety which influence how people deal with waste packaging in the home seem to diminish in strength with distance from the 'core' of the house – the living areas. This may map across actual distance, or it may be to do with the strength of the distinctions between categories of spaces.

As we saw above, different rules seem to apply to packaging re-use in different types of garden – the same assumptions about what types of object are fitting do not apply to flower gardens and to vegetable gardens. Allotment gardens for growing vegetables are often quite a long way from where the people who use them live and a different set of standards govern how to manage material objects in them. They are doubly distant from the rules of domestic propriety that govern how packaging is managed in the dwelling; they belong in a different category and are separated by physical space. Allotments are consequently rich sites for re-use; the normal rules of how leftover objects and materials should be used do not apply, and therefore creativity with the material detritus of consumption can be exercised freely in them. David Crouch, in his study of the culture of everyday landscapes, notes the highly visible presence of re-used detritus, including packaging, on the distinctive visual character of allotments:

The details of this landscape are provided by the material used – women's tights and old pipes; zinc foil and cut plastic bottles; compost containers made out of recycled wood and iron bars. The sheds are likely to be home-made and exhibit the wide limit of this eccentric landscape: wooden panels, multi-coloured wood from grocery boxes, railway sleepers and window frames from refurbished houses. (Crouch, 1993, pp28–29)

Here, packaging is re-used both as material and as re-used items, along with a whole range of other types of object pressed into service as parts of a rich variety of allotment constructions – sheds, fences, raised beds, cloches, bird scarers, fruit cages. In contrast to the slight sense of shame that people associate with 'hoarding' used packaging in the home, this re-use is characterized by the enthusiastic celebration of a function fulfilled cheaply, or for free, using material that would otherwise go to waste. It draws on a tradition of thrift and self-reliance that is a characteristic of allotments in the UK and the US (Crouch, 1993).

Because it exists so far away from the run of domestic life, both spatially and in terms of the norms that apply to it, the allotment serves here not to show how packaging might be designed to be re-used but to demonstrate the existence of the parameters within which such design must operate if packaging is to be re-used close to the spatial centre of the home. Because the constraints that govern domestic space are relaxed in the allotment, their existence is all the more evident – for instance materials which would not be acceptable in domestic spaces can be put to use in allotments. The existence of these rules is demonstrated rather neatly in the image in Figure 4.7, where a garden shed, which can function as a space in which to retreat from the demands of front-stage performances, is 'dressed up' with lace curtains in its windows. These presumably serve a dual function – to make the appearance of the shed more fitting for the space it occupies near to the house and to conceal its contents from view, accentuating the fact that the inside of the shed is a space of a different class to the garden it sits in.

The interior of sheds will be considered later in this chapter, but in the meanwhile it is appropriate to consider how gardens work in relation to the houses they sit next to. Much has been made of the significance of gardens for people. In a collection of essays from 1990, Francis and Hester suggest that gardens have three types of power – as 'idea, place and action'. While this seems true of gardens, it could be said as easily of other spaces that people inhabit, such as the domestic interiors discussed earlier in this chapter. For all that, the ideas that affect the way we relate to outside spaces, gardens included, are different to those which influence us in what we do inside our homes. However, as we will shortly see, there are also significant relationships between how people deal with gardens and how they deal with their homes in general.

Figure 4.7 Dressed shed

Source: Authors

Mark Francis' research suggested that gardens benefit their owners for a range of reasons. They are a place to 'be', a place to care for growing things, a place to control, a place to exert creativity, a place that reflects personality, a place of freedom, a place for productive work, a place to own, a place that develops over time and a place of retreat (1990, p206). Some of the strongest ideas influencing our relationship with gardens derive from their connection to the concept of 'nature' – gardening is taken to be good for you because of this connection, and Rachel and Stephen Kaplan (1990) identify empirical evidence for the psychological benefit that can accrue from gardening. As with interior spaces, there are ideas about what materials are appropriate in gardens, crossing over with what is considered natural and what is not, which are likely to influence how packaging may be re-used in gardens.

The importance of gardens and gardening in our domestic arrangements is indicated by the fact that at the end of the 20th century people in the UK spent 67 million pounds every week creating and looking after them.[9] The concern about and care for gardens that this spending indicates draws on deep cultural roots, and has particular inflections that relate to the quality of our times. A study by Mark Bhatti and Andrew Church reviews the theoretical background to gardening – the ideas that may influence it as a practice – as well as identifying which types of people garden and the reasons they give for it. In the 1990s, 48 per cent of the UK population were active gardeners. Of this gardening half of the population, a majority are older and wealthier people – 61 per cent of 60–69 year olds garden against 21 per cent of 20–24 year olds and 60 per cent of those gardening are in higher income groups against 40 per cent in lower income groups. These figures suggest that 'for a significant proportion of the adult population the garden is an important domestic space and perhaps a fifth of adults are garden "lovers" who place a very high value on the garden' (Bhatti and Church, 2004, p43).

The nature of what people do in gardens has changed over recent decades, along with a general reduction in the size of individual private gardens. This has led to a reduction in vegetable growing in favour of lawns and flowers, and Bhatti and Church suggest that along with this has gone an increase in 'packaged' gardening influenced by consumerism – what they call a 'containerized' approach to gardening determined by what is available at garden centres. The importance of gardens for 'making a house into a home' markedly outweighs any environmentalist rationale for gardening – suggesting that the social mores that influence gardening practices tend to reflect those that govern the arrangement of the household generally, while concern for nature, though present in feelings about gardening, is not the strongest influence on what people do in them.

Despite this sense that gardens are now seen as extensions of the home that must be furnished in an equivalent way, Bhatti and Church did find some evidence that the garden can still operate as a 'free' space in which people can engage sensually with their surroundings, possibly to some extent outside the constraints of consumerism. Their research showed that people value their gardens as a space for 'pottering about', for a sort of un-directed work which by extension may include material exploration and creativity in a parallel to the relatively free relationship to things that is visible in allotments. The fact that packaging seems to be quite readily re-used in gardens may be significant in itself. The function of gardens as a place where people do work that is good for them – mentally and physically – provides a parallel narrative to the consumerist 'ready-made' gardening ethic.

These somewhat anti-consumerist elements in people's relationship to gardens relate to the ideas of self-reliance that are part of the gardening tradition (Crouch, 1993) and which seem naturally to connect with the creativity necessary to see new uses in used packaging. They might therefore be the basis for packaging design for re-use in the spaces of the garden, and also perhaps in other spaces in the home – kitchen, bathroom and living room. But the sequence of steps necessary for re-use in the garden takes in the hidden spaces related to the garden, the equivalent of the hidden twilight

Figure 4.8 Messy shed interior

Source: Authors

zones discussed above, that might be found behind the lace curtains in Figure 4.7. Because they are back-stage spaces, the insides of sheds and garages may have no pretensions for display; they may be simply temporary dumping grounds for material that is marginal to everyday life. The scene in Figure 4.8 contains some packaging, some of it re-used but much of it simply left over, discarded.

It would be a mistake, however, to think that the passive attitude to this 'between space' that is implied by the unkempt appearance of these shelves is a characteristic of all such spaces. Standards for tidiness extend here as well, and at the extreme sheds, garages, workshops and other areas of the dwelling outside the living space can be highly ordered, sometimes employing packaging to provide that order. Figure 4.9 shows an array of shelves where large laundry detergent containers have been used to create bins for storing small household supplies. Clearly this arrangement required a good deal of commitment, to save the containers, to modify them and to arrange the shelving to make them accessible. The affordance for this secondary use exists in the containers, in that they are strong enough to withstand it, but the person making the arrangement required commitment, motivated by a desire to save

Figure 4.9 Tidy shed interior

Source: Authors

waste driven by thrift or environmental concern. Re-using the containers in this way also required creativity and meant they needed to be prepared to modify their habits and routines as well as the physical arrangement of their home to create and maintain the 'system' that provides the containers with their new function.

Conclusion

This chapter has provided the third element in understanding the context for packaging re-use – the spaces and routines through which it happens. It has built on the previous chapters covering the influence of the physical make-up of packaging on its re-use and the dispositions that people bring to the process. The next chapter will consider how design can bring these elements together. It takes into account the flows of packaging through the home and the points at which this gets arrested in twilight zones as well as the creativity and constraints that influence re-use. The norms and expectations about the proper use and management of objects in the different spaces of the domestic environment and their relationship to individuals' habits will be brought together to form a set of outline principles for designing for re-use.

Notes

1   There are a large number of potential uses for yoghurt pots – suggestions for re-use from www.recyclethis.co.uk/20071221/how-can-i-re-use-or-recycle-yoghurt-pots include candle moulds, containers for small screws and nails, freezing small quantities of food, starting seeds, children's paint pots, dog-food containers, ice-lolly moulds, and tofu press.

2   Walter's later book (2005) suggests quite starkly that the inside of our homes is a direct expression of the inside of our minds; a cluttered home is apparently the product of an unhealthy mind. The cleansing of 'clutter' from the home is supposed to accompany the restoration of control over one's life; our physical surroundings are taken to be a reflection of our mental state. Both when concentrating on the home specifically and on 'lifestyle' more generally, including mental life, it is the form of interior arrangements that is stressed as their important factor – whether they look tidy. The associations that our possessions have for us are not taken to be important; we should be ever ready to be made anew. It is beyond the scope of this book to consider the psychological basis for such an assumption, or the range of its potential consequences. One possible consequence of the life-laundry ethic is that a home cleared of 'junk' (whether sold, passed to friends/family or 'junked' – in other words discarded) becomes a convenient vessel for a new set of possessions. However, Gregson et al (2007b) suggest that to see the divestment of goods as a straightforward driver for consumption ignores the complexity that exists in how people get rid of unwanted goods, where, why and when.

3   Cwerner and Metcalfe's article is quite short and implies that the same values accrue from de-cluttering and from storage. There certainly does seem to be a relationship between the literature that promotes de-cluttering as bringing psychological benefits and similar literature that promotes clever devices for storing items not required to be immediately accessible. However, in the context of a de-cluttering operation, there is presumably a continuum in the decisions about what to do with items that clutter, ranging from disposing of them in some way – getting them out of the house either to waste or to another owner – and storing them in the house out of the way. If so, then the same benefits should presumably be ascribed to both storage and disposal in the literature. It would be interesting to know whether this is the case. Noting Gregson et al's recent work (2007a) questioning the notion that we live in a 'throw-away' society, it would seem that a distaste for waste and the value placed on the common practice of saving possessions and finding further owners for them are likely to be responsible for quite a different orientation to storage than to disposal.

4   There would also be changes in the physical character of the tin – the unpainted surfaces would tarnish, the colour darkening. The painted surfaces would chip and wear with use, dulling the crispness of the graphics.

5   See, for example, a discussion of the building of an authentic identity in the elite wine market (Beverland, 2005).

6   This is a much simplified version of Postrel's scheme.

7   Clement Greenberg's 1939 article in *Partisan Review*, 'Avant-garde and kitsch', is responsible for making 'kitsch' a familiar word in intellectual discourse. He offered the following definition of kitsch:

> *Kitsch, using for raw material the debased and academicized simulacra of genuine culture, welcomes and cultivates this insensibility. It is the source of its profits. Kitsch is mechanical and operates by formulas. Kitsch is vicarious experience and faked sensations. Kitsch changes according to style, but remains always the same. Kitsch is the epitome of all that is spurious in the life of our times. Kitsch pretends to demand nothing of its customers except their money – not even their time. (Greenberg, 1939, p37)*

8   The prevalence of tin collecting is indicated by the fact that a search for internet sites related to 'collectables tins' in the UK turned up over 120,000 results in May 2009.

9   The 67m pounds we spend on gardens per week breaks down in this way:

	Average weekly household expenditure (£)	Total weekly expenditure (£ million)
Garden equipment – barbecues, lawn mowers, wheel barrows	0.3	6.0
Garden tools and accessories	0.2	5.0
Garden furniture	0.2	4.0
Horticultural goods, plants, flowers	2.1	52.0

It compares to 66 million pounds spent per week on fresh fruit and nuts, 47 million on sweets and chocolate, 56 million on meals at school and work, 72 million on medicines and spectacles, 63 million on cosmetics and hair products, and 75 million on new car loans (source: British Household Expenditure Survey 1999–2000, Office of National Statistics, available at www.statistics.gov.uk/STATBASE/xsdataset.asp?vlnk=3191, accessed May 2009).

5

Re-use Practices and Design

Introduction

If the container did not have all the printing embedded into the plastic, but rather a peel-away label/removable ink, the small package would certainly be considered cute enough to re-use and, if the product is effective, the item would be purchased again – for both the product and the packaging.

This is a quote from personal correspondence with an individual who lives on the west coast of the US. The authors contacted her because she is a committed re-user – the storage area of her 'craft room' is shown in Figure 4.9. Her comment about a pack that she likes, but does not find easy to re-use because it has printing on it that she cannot remove, points towards many of the themes which this chapter will cover. The pack could have been designed differently, with removable printing. She calls the pack 'cute' – she has a notable personal relationship with it that she suggests could include re-use if it were designed differently. This chapter will consider how people make such relationships with packaging and how design can facilitate them.

The previous chapters have thought in turn about the what, who and where of re-use: the materials that packaging is made from, the dispositions that people have that affect whether they re-use it and the domestic spaces that are relevant to re-use. This chapter brings these elements together to consider how it is possible to work with the inventiveness that we have seen in play in the previous chapters as people re-use packaging to promote more re-use of more types of packaging to reduce the resources we consume. It introduces elements that have not been emphasized so far, particularly the potential for design to be an integrating force between the ways that packaging flows through people's homes and the ways that its formal elements – its shape, material and structure – can facilitate re-use. The chapter reviews more examples that demonstrate how widespread re-use is and implies that if people can find so many ways of re-using objects as simple as yoghurt pots and drink bottles, further functions for other types of packaging may lurk undiscovered. If these examples are taken as evidence for a spontaneous up-flowing of enthusiasm for re-use, they could be the basis for collaboration between consumers and designers that takes advantage of the everyday creativity that the examples demonstrate to make packaging re-use a conventional part of our everyday lives.

A number of recent approaches to designing extend outside the professional enclave to include non-designers – as users, consumers, mass-customizers, experiencers of technology, co-designers and even, as we saw in Chapter 1, simply people. It is appropriate to consider which of the principles that these approaches to design have developed might make a useful basis from which to promote packaging re-use. This chapter identifies an approach to designing that fits with the ways that people re-use packaging. This is not a top-down style of designing, where consumers are the passive recipients of the offerings of professionals qualified to provide ready-made technical solutions to their problems. Nor is this sort of designing dependent on especially gifted designers who can use their unique creative 'magic' to inspire consumers' desire by playing on the system of fashion. It has more in common with the collaborative, participative, 'co-design' approaches that have emerged out of architecture and interaction design.

This chapter shows that people who come up with ways to re-use packaging take advantage of the power of contemporary communication technology to share and disseminate their ideas. The philosophy behind this book is to work with the elements of consumer packaging re-use that emerge spontaneously from people's everyday activities, and using communication technology to disseminate re-use ideas is now one of these elements. This means that an approach to designing that is appropriate for packaging re-use will also take advantage of this type of communication. People communicate avidly online about a whole slew of different activities that involve interacting with objects and environments, and many of these interactions are not part of the conventional processes of production, consumption and dispossession. Such interventions could be collective if they used the networked communication that is available online. Many videos can be found posted online where people show each other how to complete tasks ranging from silver-soldering to pastry-making. This communication is evidence of an economy of knowledge exchange that overlaps with, but is distinct from, the commercial and academic mainstream and is located in people's private lives.

These diverse virtual networks include the exchange of ideas about re-using consumer packaging – though this has to be disentangled from the many discussions about recycling that also take place, as noted in Chapter 1, as well as industry-focused discussions of remanufacturing and re-use. From the evidence provided by the online communication that does relate to the subject of this book, it is possible to see that re-using consumer packaging satisfies a combination of needs that reflect some of the elements of re-use identified in previous chapters. It is clear that one motivation is to achieve the satisfaction that results from creating something useful by dint of effort and creativity, through craft. It is also clear that for some people this satisfaction is amplified by the sense that in re-using packaging they have done something that fits with an environmentalist ethic. This ethic suggests that to re-use packaging is a good because it diverts material from the waste stream and reduces the consumption of resources in new products. This position on re-use exists in the context of strong shared anxiety about the relationship between our current levels of consumption and environmental damage that may lead to catastrophe.

This chapter starts by thinking about the qualities of packaging objects themselves that may facilitate or inhibit re-use.

Open and Closed Objects; Fixity and Fluidity for Up-cycling

The previous chapters have pointed towards a basic quality of packaging designs that facilitate re-use, summing this quality up as 'openness'. It is worth looking at this concept in some depth here because it connects with aspects of re-use that fall on both sides of the production/consumption border – it can be kept in mind when packaging is designed and it also seems to be part of what people respond to when they find further uses for packaging. Chapter 1 discussed some of the many further uses people find for plastic carrier bags, some of which have been exposed by the restriction in supply of free bags in response to calls to 'ban the plastic bag'. These further uses take advantage of affordances that are latent in the simple format of carrier bags, which is common to the many variations on the basic type. While a carrier is a simple object because of its simple format, the variety of specific forms in which it appears and its thorough integration into everyday practices seem to combine to help people find a startling variety of further uses for it.

Some of the variations on the intended functions of plastic carrier bags to carry (goods) and communicate (brands) that are evident in their re-use were introduced in Chapter 1. Using carriers as liners for waste bins or for carrying dog mess to a bin are not the end of the story, however, as most people's experience probably suggests. Carrier bags are found re-used to protect people's possessions from dirt and damp environments, to pack objects in transit, to seal and insulate draughty houses, as emergency rainwear or temporary gloves, and as hanging containers for growing plants, all of which re-uses rely on the 'openness' of their physical design. Plastic carrier bags are objects and can be re-used as such, fixed in their 'proper' function, but they are such minimal objects that they are easy to convert into a material that can be made into something else – in other words they can be up-cycled. Their ubiquity means that this material is abundantly available and some examples of people finding uses for it are discussed below.

This range of re-uses for carrier bags as objects and as material seem to consist in affordances that are available in the bag's flexibility, both the physical flexibility of its material and the fact that its ubiquity means it is able to insinuate itself into many settings without being out of place. Many carrier bags have visual as well as physical 'content' and, as we saw with the Netto carriers in Chapter 1, this can influence whether people are willing to re-use them in situations where they will be on display to others. So the re-use potential in carrier bags as bags has a physical dimension – they must be physically up to the job we intend for them – and a cultural one – we must be able to stand re-using them. What a packaging object like a carrier bag means to us can constitute a cultural barrier to re-use or it can facilitate it. The Netto brand image may make some people less willing to re-use their carriers, just as Harrods' brand image may make some people more willing to re-use theirs.

The way that the meaning of packaging objects affects their re-use is paradoxical in a more structural sense too. While all objects are in principle culturally 'open' – their meanings shift and change along with changes in culture – at a particular time and place such meanings do have the power they happen to have. It is possible to imagine packaging objects where re-use is closed off because of the meaning they carry – extreme examples that come to mind might draw on cultural taboos based on the powerful effect of the non-physical aspects of objects. It would be unlikely, for instance, for someone to re-use the packaging in which they received a loved one's ashes from the crematorium.[1] Less extreme, but possibly also powerful, is the inhibiting effect on re-use if packaging is directed at a cultural group to which the potential re-user does not belong – a simple matter of the brand values which are communicated through the packaging design not matching the concerns of the potential re-user. The product might, for instance, be aimed at a group at a different life stage – the young person referred to in Chapter 1 not wishing to re-use a particular carrier bag for school is a case in point.[2]

However, *because* the meaning of a piece of packaging is not fixed, it can be possible to facilitate its re-making in re-use by using design to alter its meaning, or to make it easier for re-users to alter it. The products of the Doy Bags Co-op in the Philippines are an example of the re-making of the meaning of packaging through design. Although they are not an example of re-use that strictly fits the central remit of this book, because they are commercialized and emerge from a social enterprise rather than from the creative actions of individuals in their homes, they serve to demonstrate the way that the flexibility of the meaning of packs can feed into their re-use.

The Doy Bags Co-Op[2] is made up of over 500 people in the Philippines, mainly female breadwinners, who produce a range of bags, purses and jewellery from consumer packaging and other waste. The bags are sold by mail order across the world and most of them are made from used juice packs that are collected and processed. Some are made from pre-consumer waste from the juice packers to supplement the supply of used material. The graphic style of the juice packs – colourful, text-rich and distinctively Southeast Asian – is prominent in many of the designs, giving the resulting bags a distinct identity. What they mean to consumers has two aspects, one ethical and one environmental. The geopolitical and economic relationship between where they are

Figure 5.1 Doy Bag made of re-used juice packs

Source: Authors

produced and where they are consumed, the fact that they are produced in the poor South of the globe and consumed in the rich North, combined with their 'fair-trade' credentials, gives consuming the bags a charitable gloss. The bags' identity also invokes the environmental benefit of re-using packaging based in a critique of wasteful consumption. But the bright, carnivalesque visual character of the packaging they are made from, combined with the geographical and cultural distance between their producers and consumers, means their identity also perhaps includes an element of ironic play on consumerism, perhaps even a celebration of it.

Just as recycling can be seen as a validation of disposability (Lucas, 2002) – it is OK to be wasteful if you recycle your waste – because Doy Bags are made of re-used juice packs, they may in a similar way allay the anxieties of the privileged northern-hemisphere consumer about wasteful packaging, their own as well as that produced in other parts of the world. Because at least some packaging waste is made into attractive products which we can also consume, this consumption somehow seems to neutralize its own ill effects. The value of up-cycling these juice packs to the co-op members can not be denied, and the radical recasting of their meaning that it brings about demonstrates the mutability and flexibility of the meaning of all packaging. The former is a genuine ethical good, and the latter is a valuable principle to note in the context of efforts to design for the re-use of any packaging. However, the geographical and cultural distance between where the bags are produced and where they are consumed may also serve to distance consumers from the problem of packaging waste: they are from a space inhabited by 'others' rather than by 'us', a space of fantasies, holidays and dreams rather than everyday realities. Their ironic style retrieves the juice packs from the murky guilt-infested waters of waste and transforms their material from being part of a problem into a palliative for the conscience of those who consume them that plays along with the assumption that we can overcome the ecological problems created by our consumption by continuing to consume, but with a conscience.

Design to Facilitate Re-use – Shape and Labelling

The mutability of the meaning of packaging, its flexibility, is as relevant to the re-use of post-consumer re-use in people's homes in the northern hemisphere as it is to the Doy Bags example. The meaning of packaging in everyday life can also be re-cast from problem to opportunity, from commodity to possession, from waste to raw material, and this can be facilitated by its design. The person doing the re-using requires a particular orientation, which will be explored later in this chapter in connection with some examples, but it also can be aided by physical features designed into the packaging. These are so simple as to almost not need stating, but the fact that they are not universal features of packaging designs means that it is appropriate to identify them here. The practices of everyday life through which packaging flows and in which its meanings are made consist of ideas and actions – feelings and physical facts – and to facilitate re-use, design must acknowledge and engage with both, and both are always on the move. Just as culture changes, so do the requirements for the physical functions to which re-used packaging may be put.

To stay for a moment with the physical rather than the cultural aspects of packaging that facilitate or inhibit re-use, we saw in previous chapters that arresting the flow of packaging through the home to make it possible to re-use it often involves periods when it occupies a twilight zone while it acquires a new purpose. These twilight zones are real physical spaces, in real homes, where space is often at a premium, and therefore to design packaging to rest easily in such spaces is to facilitate re-use. It is a simple principle, but packs that nest inside each other may be easier to keep for a period simply because several of them take up little more space than a single one – food containers are a good example of this. The yoghurt pots in Figure 4.3 nest inside each other and are conveniently stored near to where they are processed in the kitchen. Adopting the language of the kitchen as factory (Lupton and Miller, 1992), their design allows them to fit easily into the flow of actions related to provisioning the home and sorting the waste that this produces.

Whether or not it is easy to store packs is perhaps an obvious physical aspect of their design with implications for their re-use. It operates entirely on a practical level – packs that take up too much space are less likely to be re-used. Other aspects of the physical design of packaging have implications for re-use that relate to their integration into people's 'extended self' (Belk, 2008).

The earlier chapters of this book demonstrated the relationship between packaging re-use and the presentation of self. The way that acquiring and displaying possessions can signal to others something about their owner's personality or their wealth has been understood since the early 20th century. Colin Campbell (2005) gives an account of a shift in the perception of this relationship between consuming and the self from one which took consumption to be in the service of a pre-existent self to one which recognizes that one of the consequences of the work of consumption is the self as an ongoing project – we do not simply choose the things we consume to reflect our character and personality; it is partly though choosing our possessions and our subsequent interactions with them that we construct and confirm our sense of ourselves. This happens in a number of spheres of consumption, including clothes, as Sophie Woodward's ethnographic work on how women make their everyday clothes choices shows (2007). The earlier chapters demonstrated that people's actions with packaging – particularly when they re-use it for some purpose or other – can also have a relationship with their ongoing project of the self, whether packaging is re-used inside the house or in the garden, for a physical purpose or for display.

Because re-use is not a conventional type of consumption – it is the reverse of consumption in the sense of 'using up' – it might be expected that aspects of the relationship between the self identity of a re-user and the packaging objects they re-use would also be different. Although the display of packaging – its use as props for the front-stage performance of self – is equivalent to the display of other types of goods, any time packaging is modified so it can be re-used, it acquires quite a different relationship to self-identity. It ceases to be an object from which someone is more or less alienated – something that is more or less of a possession – and becomes something they have created:

it becomes in a sense a craft object. The process of re-formation may require a change in the object itself, but in the process the person's relationship to it is also radically altered and the ways people make physical changes to the pack that relate to this relationship seem particularly significant. People often seem to want to erase the evidence on the pack of its origin as a commodity before they are easy with re-using it – in doing this they seem to want to render it 'neutral' so they can turn it into a possession that has the same sort of relationship to their self-identity as something they have made, that they have crafted. This 'opening up' of a piece of packaging, being able to remove its commodity meaning so that it can be brought into a relationship with the self, seems to facilitate some re-use. For example, the mozzarella container in Figure 3.8 is less 'open' to re-use in this respect because its meaning cannot be changed – the fact that it will carry its branding into any further use to which it is put may be a barrier to its re-use. On the other hand, among the most familiar re-used packaging items are jam jars, and the design of jar that the authors' research has shown to be particularly re-usable is particularly easy to 'neutralize', because it is easy both to clean the jar and to completely remove the label.

This barrier results from the nature of the relationship that a re-user builds with a pack when they modify it for re-use or up-cycle its material. There is a sense in which such modification means the pack has to stop being an object, while remaining one. A collection of yoghurt pots stored in a twilight zone is a collection of objects, but it might end up performing as a cache of material, and this is only resolved by the particular way the pots get re-used. There is an echo in this processing – from 'closed' commodity, to 'open' re-useable objects/material, to re-used object – of the way that all the things that enter our lives as commodities have to be processed to be turned into possessions; 'domestication' is the name that sociologists have given to this transformation from commodity to possession (Kopytoff, 1986; Carrier, 1990). In the case of packaging, this transformation is particularly radical, because it is often the wrapping for products which projects their commodity status, sometimes more strongly than the products themselves. Therefore in order to be re-used, packaging has to be made to leave the world of commodities and enter the 'moral economy' of the home, as Silverstone, Hirsch and Morley call it (1992) – it has to be 'domesticated' by having its identity removed. If its identity can't be removed, it can't be domesticated and may not be re-used.

The concept of domestication has been developed in studies of how people integrate new information and communication technologies into their homes, and the process that goes on when packaging is re-used seems to be equivalent to this in some ways. People accommodate themselves to technology through a process of negotiation that incorporates it into their homes and makes it part of them. Packaging that is diverted for re-use gives up its commodity character to be re-configured for its new purpose, incorporated into the domestic space rather than ejected from it. This domestication rests partly on simply being accepted into the domestic space instead of being consigned to the bin, and partly because it is being required to behave differently than packaging normally does – it is being asked to perform. This performance is drawn out of it by a packaging re-user; it is often not an obvious performance, not one that packaging is very ready to give – further performance has to be coaxed out of the packaging.

A degree of commitment is required on the part of the re-user to do this coaxing – it is usually easier to throw packaging away than to re-use it. For this reason, perhaps, even if the re-used packaging is not going to be part of the front-stage performance of the re-user's self-identity, it seems important to be able to open up the meaning of the packaging to work with it, as well as to make use of what physical 'openness' it might have. If it is possible to remove the branding and labelling through which the pack performs as a commodity, this seems to facilitate the sort of inventive re-use that people get involved with in their homes.[3] There are three strands of evidence for this. Individuals involved in the authors' research spoke about liking to be able to remove labelling from packs in order to re-use them, and the same desire is voiced in the public discussions of re-use that take place on the internet, which will be discussed shortly.

The design of some packaging that deliberately encourages re-use, such as the Innocent food pack in Figure 5.2, also provides evidence for this desire to be able to neutralize the meaning of a pack to ready it for re-use. As well as making it easy to sort the materials used in it for recycling, the design of this pack explicitly acknowledges that re-using it is another way of dealing with it, offering suggestions for some further uses for the plastic tub. The fact that these instructions are not printed on the tub itself but on its separable card wrapper suggests that this company understands that packs which are designed to be open in this way facilitate re-use.

There is also a very practical reason for designing easily removable labels for food and drink packs that are physically capable of being re-used. This relates to the safety implications of some of the purposes to which re-used packaging may be put. For instance, it is not unusual for people to use food and drink containers to store poisonous materials, and if the packs have labelling that cannot be removed, this can have tragic consequences. The chemical safety literature contains some very sad stories about poisoning incidents involving the herbicide Paraquat, which is both a very effective weed killer and extremely poisonous to human beings and other animals. This chemical, banned in the EU since 2007 because of its toxicity, has been the poison of choice for many suicides, but has also been responsible for tragic accidental poisonings. Decanted and stored in drink bottles, because of its colour the concentrated weed killer is easily confused with a cola drink. One unfortunate individual died 25 days after mistaking Paraquat for vinegar and sprinkling it on his chips (Eisler, 2000, p1159).

Designing food and drink containers with an easily removable label, or which can have their identity as commodities easily obscured in other ways, might lessen the likelihood of such tragedies. While this reason for making packs which can be rendered symbolically neutral and open to re-formulation is compelling, it is the relationship between this openness and the likelihood that people *will* re-use packs that connects to the purpose of this book. It is easier for people to build an attachment with a pack that is symbolically neutral as a potential material for re-use. The process of building this attachment can in principle be influenced by the design of the packaging – either its form and materials or its graphic aspects, as shown in Figure 5.2. It is a relatively simple matter to design packaging that is likely to be re-used with removable labelling to allow people to develop their own attachment to it as a singular possession.

Rendering the material of packaging into useful things requires the re-user to draw on their personal resources, and this process seems to be inhibited by strong, permanent branding, as if the presence of the commodity identity of the packaging inhibits the process of developing personal attachment to

Figure 5.2 Food packaging designed for re-use

Source: Authors

the pack, because it remains too clearly an object, with all its attendant associations. It retains the 'functional fixedness' that Von Hippel identifies (1988), rather than having obvious potential for a further use. It is the fact that re-use often requires the rendering of packs into a new form, using them as material for crafting into a new object, which seems to bring about this attachment. Craft processes are commonly understood to result in objects that are defined by attachment not alienation. Colin Campbell identifies some of the assumptions about what craft processes are like and their defining features. He suggests that in the writings of Marx and Veblen craft is seen as 'ennobling, humanizing and … the ideal means through which individuals could express their humanity' (Campbell, 2005, pp24–25) and cites Tanya Harrod (1995) for a definition of craft as 'made and designed by the same person'. The re-use of packaging requires creative input from the re-user and often some physical modification of the pack. It is craft by Harrod's definition, and the potential of craft to offer satisfaction and fulfilment means that some re-users seem intrinsically motivated to re-use – they don't need much encouragement. They also seem ready to communicate about their re-use through various internet-based forums, to which we now turn our attention.

Online Re-use

In 2005 a multidisciplinary group formed a web-based company called Instructables, a site where 'passionate people share what they do and how they do it, and learn from and collaborate with others'.[4] Some members of this group had studied at MIT's Media Lab and formed a consortium called Squid Labs, out of which the Instructables idea grew, along with other firms. The concept of Instructables is that members can post instructions on how to make or do something, to share their knowledge and receive comment from other members on it. The range of somethings that people posted on the site was at first clustered round electronics-related projects, but now includes categories such as cooking, art, craft, games, 'green' and sports. There is also a section called 'life', which includes subcategories on babies, Mother's Day and exercise – it seems there can be a useful set of instructions relating to all aspects of life. The site runs contests such as, at the time of writing, one on the art of sound and one titled 'get in the garden'. A recent contest was titled 'keep the bottle', intended to prompt members to share ways of re-using plastic drink bottles, which attracted 170 entries that included ideas for turning drink bottles into lamps, using them for pranks, and as components for an algae bioreactor and a hydroponic system. The winning entries were a guide for how to use a plastic bottle to fashion a prosthetic arm and one for turning them into attractive swimming buoys, shown in Figure 5.3.

Figure 5.3 Plastic bottle buoy

Source: Authors

A search for 're-use' on the Instructables website turns up many more examples of packaging re-use. These include instructions for re-using items ranging from 55-gallon drums to crisp packets, though many of the instructions are for uses for plastic drink bottles. These uses for drink cans, bottles, boxes, bags, tins, tissue paper and yoghurt pots all demonstrate a measure of creativity in varying degrees. However, in even the most obvious suggestion for re-using these packaging items, there is a significant degree of commitment and enthusiasm – reflected in many cases in the comments that other members can post below each 'instructable'.[5] It is in this feature of the site that the greatest potential exists for promoting and encouraging re-use, because the solidarity it indicates strongly counters the commodity identity of packaging and may open up the possibility of an ethic of re-use. Many of the instructables to do with packaging re-use point to revising the systems of provision for some goods, as well as ameliorating their effects by re-using packaging. For example, there is more than one instructable about re-using plastic drink bottles which has attracted comments that recommend popularizing drinking tap water to reduce the number of used bottles produced.

The members of the Instructables Network, or 'documentation platform' as its CEO Eric Willhelm terms it, are not typical consumers. They are not part of the mainstream and the Instructables site does not come out of the mainstream. Rather, it seems to have emerged from the minds of the future intellectual leaders of the world – the MIT Media Lab is famous for its reputation for developing new technologies and outlining future visions. The impact of the Instructables interventions may be limited by this exclusivity, and also by the avowedly wacky character that some of them have, but it is not the only web-based entity that may influence change in our practices with packaging waste, its creation as well as its re-use. There are blogs about re-using plastic bottle waste to make flowers[6] as well as the ManyOne portal network – a public service site that includes an Earth, Nature and Environment portal with a community devoted entirely to up-cycling waste into fashion, furniture, art and architecture,[7] much of that waste being waste packaging.

The examples on the ManyOne portal network are rather different from the packaging up-cycling and re-use instructables. The members of Instructables may, like the founders of the site, have advanced qualifications and be talented scientists and engineers but the site has a make-do-and-mend spirit, dedicated to sharing ways of solving problems close to home, close to the practice of everyday life. The results are often not spectacular, in fact in some cases it is quite difficult to be very enthusiastic about them as ideas for re-use that could be widely adopted, but the significant thing about them is that they grow out of the application of creativity to a personal need using the materials that are at hand. In contrast, ManyOne offers upmarket up-cycling. The examples it shows are the work of concerned professionals – artists, fashion designers and architects. What is immediately apparent from the examples of up-cycled waste that these practitioners have turned into art, clothes, products and buildings is that, along with their undoubted environmental concern, they bring their professional values to these projects. This means, understandably, that they concentrate on objects as solutions, wrought according to varying configurations of the values of high design. They offer objects as remedies for the problem of waste, which means they place rather less emphasis on engaging with the practices that create the waste in the first place.

For this reason, despite the avant-garde appearance of some of the design solutions that come out of the eco-design community that are represented on the ManyOne portal network, it is Instructables that may show the way forward. For all that a beautifully crafted ball gown made from the plastic that protects sheets of plate glass or the dress made from ring pulls shown in Figure 5.4 may be spectacular, and their existence and promotion is likely to raise awareness of waste materials and may inspire some individuals to take positive action, it is the members of Instructables who are harbingers of re-formed practices with packaging. They are revising their own relationships to the materiality of packaging, and to many other technologies.

Figure 5.4 Dress made from ring-pulls

Source: Haute Trash

The fact that the results of the efforts of those posting instructables are often unspectacular may indicate the power of this online network to contribute to changing the way that we live with material objects, packaging included, rather than being a failing. The lack of spectacle in the instructables seems not to be random, but to derive from an ethic as deeply ingrained as the highly aestheticized approach evident in the examples of up-cycling waste that can be found via the ManyOne portal. This is a community of people many of whom seem at home with the most advanced engineering and technology, in whom values of thrift and self-reliance combine with technical competence, creativity and pro-environmental attitudes. From the point of view of efforts to promote the re-use of packaging, it is tempting to wonder whether this community represents a set of leaders along the lines of Von Hippel's 'lead users'. Clearly, however, the term does not fit this group perfectly, since they are also inventing the products that they are using. There is more overlap between them and the 'user-innovators' modifying mountain bikes described by Luthje, Herstatt and Von Hippel (2005). It is the relationship between the inventive processes, the resulting products and the everyday practices in which they fit that may make the members of Instructables a potent force for change.

The Concept of 'Practice'

It seems that both the creativity of particular individuals and communication about this creativity online may be significant in changing our practices with packaging by opening up possibilities for re-use. While it is relatively easy to see this possibility from the examples discussed here, it is not so easy to see what sort of structural or design interventions might facilitate and amplify these incipient changes. For this reason, it is worth clarifying what we mean by the concept of 'practice' when thinking about packaging, in order to more clearly specify how what we do with packaging might change in response to design.

In recent sociology, 'practice' is an inclusive term that encompasses all the aspects of a specific pattern of life – both the structural aspects that individuals cannot change and the aspects that rely on individuals' actions. The practices that involve packaging are practices of consumption – ranging from food consumption to the consumption of electronic goods. The examples discussed above, and most of the instructables that involve packaging re-use, involve finding alternative uses for packaging generated by products that are of a similar size to each other and that therefore have the same physical relationship to the human body and our living spaces. This is packaging for food and drink, clothes, household goods, and portable technology, which are bought frequently enough to create the flow of packaging discussed in previous chapters. Furniture, white goods, sports equipment and other types of goods all require packaging, but they are in a different category simply because these products are larger and bought less frequently, so their packaging follows a different route through the home if it enters it at all.

The consumption practices that concern us relate to items characterized as 'fast-moving consumer goods' – goods that are quickly consumed with supplies regularly replenished. The way packaging fits into the consumption of these goods has been covered in detail in previous chapters; here a brief review of practice theory provides another view of how we work with this type of packaging that integrates the material, human and spatial aspects covered in previous chapters. Clearly, a practice theory view is not the only one it is possible to take to try to understand packaging and its re-use – each of the approaches above gives useful insights into how we deal with packaging – but the degree to which a practice theory approach can integrate these approaches makes it particularly useful. Kennedy and Krogman (2008, pp182–183) review the approaches to consumerism that may be of use to efforts to promote its sustainability and see practice theory as a way to compensate for the partial view provided by thinking about it in terms of either social structures or aspects of individual personality.

What happens to consumer packaging, and what it does, results from inter-relationships between human actions, cultural knowledge and packaging objects themselves, which evolves, as we have seen. The nature of packaging and how we interact with it, its human and non-human elements, its manufacturing/production, its relationship to people's bodies, its relationship to our living spaces, develop and change together. It is not possible to influence the environmental impact of the whole system, or even adequately to understand it, by concentrating on only one of its parts (Shove, 2006). In her analysis of what we take to be normal in our material surroundings, Elizabeth Shove (2003, p48) identifies three categories in play in such a set of relationships. The first she calls 'socio-technical systems' or 'collective conventions and arrangements'. In the case of packaging, these are the arrangements for the production, transport and selling of goods, as well as the ways our homes are organized – the kitchen as factory, for instance – and the ways our domestic waste is collected and disposed of. Her next category collects together the 'habits, practices and expectations of users and consumers' and points towards all the diverse ways people interact with and deal with packaging that have been introduced above. The word 'expectations' is particularly significant here, given the well-established expectation that packaging is valueless and should be treated as waste. Shove's third category includes qualities of objects themselves, which conventionally come within the remit of design, the 'symbolic and material qualities of socio-technical devices/objects'.

Shove's categories point towards the characterization of social practices provided by Andreas Reckwitz (2002). His summary of the aspects of practices that are 'carried' by our human activities identifies them as a 'routinized type of behaviour' consisting of the following interconnected elements:

> Forms of bodily activities, forms of mental activities, 'things' and their use, a background knowledge in the form of understanding, know-how, states of emotion and motivational knowledge. (Reckwitz, 2002, p251)

Reckwitz's characterization emphasizes the aspects of practices that are sustained through the influence of our everyday routines, rather than through norms and rational choices. It points to the fact that our ways of doing things, our practices, are sustained by what we do out of habit, without necessarily thinking about it much, if at all. Many of our actions with packaging are of this sort – the decision to save a piece of packaging for another use is a disruption to its normal flow through the home, and this normal flow is sustained in part by our habits. They are examples of the 'embedded and inter-dependent practices and habits' that Shove and Warde (1997) say are characteristic of unspectacular, hidden or 'inconspicuous' consumption.

This characterization, this emphasis on habits, downplays the structural aspects of practices – the 'socio-technical systems' that Shove points to. Our individual actions with objects cannot influence the system which is diffused into our everyday environment through the design of packaging. But while we cannot directly influence the 'collective conventions and arrangements' that mean we end up carrying home tens of kilos of plastic, glass, metal and carton board every year, in re-using packaging we are in a sense subverting the system into which it is built, particularly the assumption that we will integrate this material into our everyday habits by processing it and disposing of it as waste. It is not easy to see whether such relatively minor subversions of the system of provision are significant in themselves from the point of view of lessening the environmental impact of packaging, but Reckwitz suggests that practices change through what he calls 'ruptures' in the routines that sustain them. The dissemination and popularization of such small subversions of the system of provision, facilitated by the potential for communication that is evident through online networks, combined with packaging designs that are sensitive to the potential for re-use, might constitute such a rupture.

If we accept the synthesizing, practice-orientated view outlined above, we also accept that practices and things constitute each other – what we do and what we have to do it with are bound together with habits, routines and expectations and appeal to standards about which we have genuinely strong feelings. We have an emotional investment in our habits – they feel right. In principle, therefore, changes in the objects, expectations and routines that currently support a system of provision that creates packaging waste, rather than providing objects that are (re-useful, might constitute a 'rupture' that folds back into the system of provision as a whole. Changed things necessarily accompany changed practices. The elements of such change that are in things rather than people can be deliberate, they can be designed and they can have an influence on us as we encounter them.

The remainder of this chapter will concentrate on designing to facilitate re-use. First, some examples of design for packs that are intended to have a second use will be described. One of these is a prototype that illustrates some of the principles identified above; the others are for products that are aimed at an environmentally aware audience – people whose ideas may not need changing, but whose actions might. The chapter ends with a discussion of some of the approaches to designing that have emerged over the past 20 years, reviewing their relevance for packaging re-use.

Designs for Re-use

The psychologist Ives Kendrick (1942, p48) suggested that alongside having an 'instinct to master' the material world, people desire things they know how to use, know how to get something out of. If I can't drive, I am less likely to desire a car; if I can't swim, I may not desire a pool. Given that re-using falls within the category of 'use', it makes sense that people might also desire things they know how to re-use. Gaining re-use 'know-how' is therefore an important element in the process of individuals coming to re-use things that they may previously have thrown away, and in the case of packaging is also a potential route to stimulating consumers' desire for the products that the packaging contains. We have seen earlier in this chapter examples of re-use know-how emerging from a networked group of people communicating online – re-use innovations originating with one person's inventiveness diffusing through the network. This learning by example, through networked communication, might be complemented, and reinforced, through the design of packaging.

Figure 5.2 shows an Innocent food package that consists of a polypropylene container with a replaceable lid inside a cardboard sleeve. In its overall format, the design does not differ very significantly from a conventional pack for soup and other types of prepared food that are to be reheated. These are often packaged in similar polypropylene tubs, though in many cases there is no card sleeve but the brand information and cooking instructions are printed on a label that is stuck to the container. As we saw above, this one has been designed so that as well as being easily separated for recycling, the card sleeve carries some instructions about how the pack might be re-used, along with the usual branding, corporate copy, and cooking and safety instructions. The text on the pack in Figure 5.2 notes that recycling plastic is problematic because the provision of facilities for it varies and it suggests using the pot as a temporary goldfish bowl. Other suggestions for re-uses printed on these card sleeves have included using the pot as a mini herb garden, as a floating snack container to use in the bath, as a cereal bowl for 'when the washing up reaches critical mass' and as a jelly mould.

This re-use-orientated approach to the pack design reflects the values that the company wants to project – it is part of the company's branding effort. The brand identity of the company means that it is important that is seen to have an ethical and considered approach to its packaging, but in this design this is taken beyond the appearance of the pack. The easily separated card sleeve and the lack of printing on the pot suggest that its designers understood something of the way that packaging re-use works, for instance the fact that graphics which cannot be removed from a container can constitute a barrier to its re-use. This design leaves openings for re-use by making it possible to neutralize the commodity identity of the pack, to 'singularize' it. Not only do these aspects of the design work with re-user creativity by allowing openings for it, the company's approach to communication with its customers by promoting email comments has a relationship to the examples of the dissemination of creativity with packaging through online communication. However, for all that there are some similarities between Innocent's approach to re-use and the cases introduced above, there are also some quite significant differences between packaging re-use that grows out of everyday practices and this design *for* re-use.

While the physical arrangement of the pack acknowledges and avoids some clear barriers to re-use, and it would be a mistake to be cynical about the company's motives for designing their packaging as they do, a critical reading of it highlights the degree to which the design as a whole may succeed in doing more to promote the company's ethical brand identity than to promote actual re-use. The explicit directions for re-use on the card sleeve may work more effectively to symbolize the company's ethical brand identity than to influence people's actions with the packaging at home. Although they certainly do not constitute a barrier to the pot being re-used, it is the fact that they are there that will benefit the company, not whether or not they are followed. The suggestions for ways to re-use the Innocent pot are relatively disconnected from the everyday practices that might give them meaning, simply because they do not emerge from those practices in the way that is so distinctive about the suggestions for re-use on Instructables.

It may be that there is nothing more that any company can do to promote re-use than Innocent is doing with this design, however keen it is to work with the values and views of the people who consume its products. Innocent *is* clearly interested in doing this and invites comments and suggestions through its website, by phone and by email, and has doubtless conducted marketing research with the types of consumers that it intends to target. Given this orientation towards its consumers' concerns both for their own health and for minimizing environmental impact from their consumption, it is interesting that the suggestions that it offers for re-using the plastic pot are not more firmly embedded in indigenous practices, and it is this that points to the limits to Innocent's interest in promoting re-use being established by its importance for their brand identity – to be seen to be doing it may be enough to support the brand identity. Being more charitable, it may be that Innocent's marketing research has shown them that the UK consumers who are likely to buy their products have limited practical interest in re-use, so more strenuous efforts to promote it through their packaging design would be futile.

Re-use was clearly part of the brief for the Dorset Cereals pack in Figure 5.5, and the re-use potential of the pack is a very strong part of the product's offer to consumers. The design is based on the potential for a cereal box to keep children busy and amused through the play of imagination and physical engagement by providing things to make. The box has instructions for a

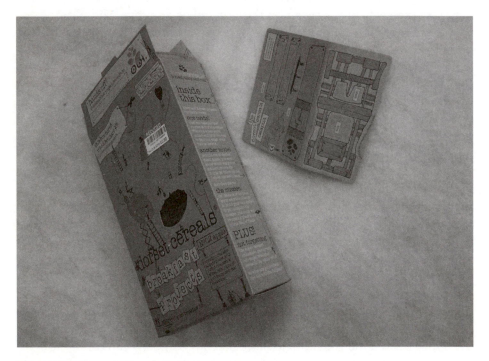

Figure 5.5 Dorset Cereals pack

Source: Authors

project printed on the inside – a Viking longship in this case – and contains a separate mini-project included inside the box. It also gives details of a competition that children can enter via the company's website to use recycled materials from the home to build a device to transport an egg three metres under its own power. There seems to be an easy relationship between playful creative engagement with materials, an ethical approach to dealing with the cereal box when it is finished with and a healthy breakfast food. All three aspects of the product have a relationship to improvement – of the mind, of the environment and of the body – categories which are likely to overlap in the market segment that is the target for this product.[8] As a sales tool, the design acknowledges that children will have an influence on which cereal a family buys, and its potential to provide children with some productive fun is likely to appeal to both children and their parents. Parents who are disposed to re-use packaging, who have a high level of environmental awareness and commitment, may also be attracted by the degree to which this design wears its re-usable heart on its sleeve, as may children who have picked up environmental messages at school.

The impact of this design on resource use is not likely to be especially great, given that the creative projects it provides are unlikely to replace the consumption of another product, though that is conceivable. What is potentially more significant about the design from the point of view of promoting re-use is that the engagement with re-use that it provides on the pack is followed through onto the company's website via a competitive element. This is intended to be more than a place to which children can submit the results of their projects: its quirky visual identity supports all the elements of the pack design in the company's engagement with child consumers. It emphasizes the immediate gratification of having re-used the box in a productive, playful way and it has a little of the potential to allow the sort of collective reflection on the creative re-use of packaging that is possible through Instructables. The children to whom it is directed would likely have a different approach to the concept of re-use than some of the members of Instructables, though there might also be some overlap – children may be more motivated by a desire for fun and imaginative play than by environmental ethics – but the re-use of packaging for fun is clearly also a motivation behind many instructables.

In both the cases just discussed, the potential for re-use is integrated into the design specifically to address an aspect of the intended market for the product – the Innocent pack uses re-use potential as part of its ethical brand identity; the Dorset Cereals pack has the further playful functions for the cereal box as the basis for making projects as a distinct selling point to both children and their parents. The next example is a conjectural design produced as part of the research that we conducted for this book and built on the insights that other aspects of the research process provided. The design is for dry powder garden fertilizer packaging, which usually takes the form of a card box with a plastic pouch or pouches inside. The re-usable design does away with the inner pouch and consists of a polypropylene box with a removable lid and a vent built into the bottom. Its intended re-use is as a cloche to protect small plants and to directly replace products that can be bought to do this. As well as having a clear secondary use, the design brings some functional benefits to its function as a fertilizer pack, in that it keeps the fertilizer dry and protected, which the current pack does not once the inner plastic pouch is opened.

The prevalence of packaging re-used in gardens, and vegetable gardens in particular, indicated that there might be a relatively easy fit between gardening practices and re-use and that this would therefore be a worthwhile environment for which to design a re-usable pack. The design is opportunistic, in that it takes account of and builds on the fact that it is common for gardeners to use plastic drink packaging as cloches or plant protectors, as we showed in Chapter 3. Re-using clear plastic containers in this way is sufficiently embedded in the practice of gardening to provide a basis on which this design can build – it develops some existing 'know-how'. The design is based on an aspect of an existing practice and takes advantage of it to extend this propensity to re-use into an aspect of a pack design that would reduce the use of resources by replacing a purchased product, with direct environmental benefit. The response of research participants to the re-designed pack was generally favourable, though some did raise the issue that the new design would be likely to cost more than the card/pouch original, noting, however, that its clear secondary use and its good fit with the needs of gardeners would be likely to outweigh a small cost premium.

For all that it was well received by research participants, this design shows up some shortcomings in this approach to designing for re-use, and consequently has some relationships to the two examples just introduced. The approach is limited in the degree to which it can connect with the spontaneous creativity of re-users, though this is partly because it was a conjectural design without the potential to plug into or create a community of re-use practice. However, it probably reflects quite well what is feasible for many manufacturers in terms of its engagement with the existing practices in which re-use fits, since this must accommodate the commercial realities of production. However, it can also draw on significant research efforts and is likely to be based, as was the design in figure 5.6, on observation research, and to use the details of the consumption practices that such research can reveal as the basis of a design intended to be re-used. The more a design is tailored for a specific further use the more closed it will be in terms of its re-use potential and this may significantly limit the environmental benefit of such designs. If gardeners happen not to need a cloche, they would not re-use the pack if this was its only possible further use. Recognizing this, this design aspires to be

Figure 5.6 Re-designed fertilizer packaging

Source: Authors

both closed and open at the same time, so its performance as a cloche does not foreclose its re-use for other purposes. The obvious other re-uses – as a container for storing things or as a planter – are only some of the re-uses that the practice of gardening would throw up for such an object.

All these examples of design for re-use have the potential to increase people's awareness of the environmental impact of packaging and therefore to promote re-use by changing attitudes. Their effect on everyday practices is, however, likely to be small, given that in the first two examples re-use is a side effect of a marketing strategy that seems primarily to be focused on building a brand that is taken to be environmentally positive. The third example takes a relatively quiet approach in comparison. The design offers the potential for a very practical re-use which would replace a purchase and which is firmly based in the practice of which the product is part, but it does not promote this as a particularly environmentally positive feature through brand identity. Because its design puts the practical benefit of re-using the pack in the foreground, rather than the 'socio-function' of being seen to be pro-environmental, it might have a better chance than the others of achieving resource saving, simply because the pack would be likely to be re-used to replace a purchase. Also, because a feature of the practice of gardening is its closeness in some cases to community relationships, in allotment societies for instance, the re-use function of this pack could be effectively disseminated by word of mouth. However, none of the examples demonstrate the leverage that online presence gives to the vigorous creativity of instructables – none of them are part of a community that can so powerfully disseminate re-uses that spontaneously arise from the practices that go on in our kitchens and gardens.

Ways of Designing Together

So far, this chapter has considered examples of design for re-use from the point of view of their relationship to the social practices with which they interlock, and it is appropriate to note the implications this may have for designing. Coherent academic study of ways of designing has a history that goes back to the mid 20th century, and arguably before that to the Bauhaus. From the Second World War, a need to increase the efficiency of the design process and the effectiveness of its results led to efforts to clarify the relationship between design problems and their solutions. These efforts drew from systematic approaches to human–machine relationships that had developed in the scientific management of production and in ergonomics and which were applied to design by organizations such as NASA. By the 1960s this work had developed into a collective enterprise distributed across the developed world that has become known as the Design Methods movement.

Nigan Bayazit (2004) reviews the development of these systematic approaches to design. He notes significant clusters of activity in the 1960s at the Royal College of Art in London and at the University of California at Berkeley, both of which applied principles from systems theory and ideas from operational research in engineering, product design and architecture. Bayazit notes that this work inherited a view of design as a 'problem-solving' activity and that this had a significant influence on the nature of the debate – a division quite quickly arose between an approach to design that sought straightforwardly to 'scientize' it using a simple model of science and a competing view that claimed that this so restricted design as to make it ineffective. The debate about the nature of design problems that went on in the Design Methods movement is of particular interest here, as is the influence on it of Horst Rittel, who held the post of Professor of the Science of Design at Berkeley from 1963 to 1990.

The environmental effects of packaging and its waste pose a particular type of problem, one that is complex and awkward. It is a problem made up of human behaviour and material elements, one that is multidetermined, having social, economic and political causes and effects. If it falls within the remit of design to engage with it, and the examples in this chapter suggest that it does, then it is an exemplary instance of the type of design conundrums that Rittel named 'wicked' problems. Wicked problems have certain char-acteristics, which Rittel first identified using that name in 1969 (see Rittel and Webber, 1973) and which were neatly summarised recently by Rith and Dubberly (2007). What is striking about Rittel's approach to design problems is that it acknowledges the fact that engaging with them involves discourse – it involves communication for deliberation and argumentation – and it is there-fore political. This insight is an observation based on the nature of wicked problems and the ways that design may 'tame' them, which emphazises that innovation has both subjective and political dimensions. There are echoes here of the tension between individual actions and social structures that is resolved, in principle at least, by the idea of social practice.

Several approaches to designing that try to respond to the wicked nature of design problems and are therefore relevant to the packaging re-use we have been discussing have emerged alongside both the Design Methods movement and reactions to it. They are sympathetic to the practices with which they engage in that they challenge the barriers that have historically existed between designers and those who use their designs – consumers and users. At its best, this type of designing can be politically radical in its challenge to the power differentials that are inscribed in the professionaliza-tion of designing, though it can also simply be a way to work out how to more quickly and effectively design products that will succeed commercially. From the early 1970s design processes involving user-participation began to appear in architecture, and since then there has been a 'turn to practice' in approaches to design that acknowledge the situated nature of experiences with information and communication technologies (McCarthy and Wright, 2004). The notion of 'participatory' design, where users are involved in the design process, has been put into practice with children in schools and museums (Hall and Bannion, 2005; Burke and Grosvenor, 2003; Burke et al, 2008) and extensively developed in architecture and computer systems design (Schuler and Namioka, 1993; Bell and Wakeford, 2008). These approaches to designing have also resulted in the breakdown of barriers between members of the different professional groups that make up design teams. They are in the spirit of the 'co-designing' that has begun to receive attention in recent years. While some of the literature relevant to this subject seems to put more stress on working across the barriers between members of design teams than on eliding the distinction between designers and users/consumers, this is not uniformly the case (Jaworski and Kohli, 2006).

The conceptual separation between design and consumption is perhaps a pragmatic response to the divisions that exist where packaging is designed and produced. Even in the most integrated cross-functional product devel-opment team (Imai et al, 1985), different individuals are concerned with how people are likely to receive a design to those who deal with the physical aspects. The marketing function is separate from the engineering function, but they are integrated by design which is able to pay close attention to how people will interact with the object. The ability of design, as the 'new liberal art of technological culture' (Buchanan, 1992, p5), to resolve apparently conflicting aspects of everyday life, such as those involved in the 'wicked problems' thrown up by packaging, reflects the relational spirit of this book; it is not possible to understand packaging waste or to use design to ameliorate its environmental effects without understanding the intersecting practices of which it is part.

However, despite the efforts of design for re-use that we have introduced above, packaging is still an issue over which we play out conflict between our apparent need for convenience and our distaste for its consequences. This suggests that design has so far failed to measure up to the task of resolving this conflict, and it is worth considering the reasons for this failure in the light of the re-use practices that we have been exploring. It may simply be that it is beyond the capability of design to address such an awkward and complex issue as the waste that packaging creates, or, taking seriously Rittel's point about taming wicked problems by agreeing on a definition of them, it may simply be that the design problem that this constitutes has not been adequately defined for it to be solved. Neither of these diagnoses rings true, however. If campaigns of war, programmes for space conquest and national infrastructure systems can be designed, then it is not beyond the wit of humans to design a system for the provision of goods that does not produce waste packaging that has no further purpose and can only be dealt with by recycling or by capturing its embodied energy or by burying it. As the early chapters of this book established, packaging with no further use is not a by-product of our system of provision, it *is* its product – it is designed *into* the system. And therefore it could be designed out.

The potential exists for design to build on the indigenous inventiveness that people exhibit, but this requires political will. Although governments have made progress in minimizing the environmental impact of packaging in recent years – the amount of packaging recycled in the UK rose from 28 per cent to 61 per cent in the decade after 1997 (Defra 2009) – the potential for re-use this book has identified remains largely unexplored. The concentration on recycling is understandable, and necessary in the circumstances, but does not capitalize on the ground–up action for packaging re-use that is evident online. A participative design ethic sits easily with the types of spontaneous action that are evident online, and, if applied to packaging re-use, could help both to define the problem and to find solutions to it. The Instructables members uploading their sometimes slightly strange ideas for re-using packaging indicate the existence of a force that has potency that is both practical and political. One of the elements of its political potency exists exactly in the degree to which this ground–up activity demonstrates the relative impotence of design efforts that come from within the professional commercial enclave to significantly alter our practices with packaging in ways that promote re-use. What is implied here is a different type of designing that transcends the relatively restricted, single-product focus of efforts to promote re-use, to encompass the system of provision in a way that fully engages with the potential for everyday practices to alter and evolve. Distaste for packaging waste already leads some of us to re-use it; the power of networked communication makes it possible for us to participate in a huge, indigenous, collective design programme, led perhaps by people with expertise like the founders of Instructables. The impediment to such a programme would be the commercial imperatives that lead to a lack of standardization in packaging designs, and it would be in enforcing standardization that government could be involved in such a collective programme.[9]

The ways that packaging gets re-used, as we have seen, depend as much on people's behaviour as on material facts. It also often involves people going against the grain of packaging – it is as much about 'system' functions as it is about 'proper' functions. We can behave differently with packaging, and this could show manufacturers and legislators how it can be re-used. For instance, if the feedback loop between the Innocent company, its packaging design and its consumers were re-modelled, there is a chance that the suggestions for re-using the polypropylene pot written on the card packaging could be more than a symbolic gesture and connect with functions that replaced purchases, and therefore reduced resource consumption. This would be a form of genuine co-designing, though it could still go further. The demand for an ethical approach to consumer packaging could affect the system of provision as a whole. Radical collective re-use disseminated online could demonstrate the potential for re-forming – re-designing – the system of provision. Re-use could, through careful design that is sensitive to the practices in which objects live, be designed in.

Summary

This chapter has sought to offer a view of ways to design for re-use that integrates the three views of packaging in the earlier chapters from the perspective of design. Bearing in mind that packaging can be considered from the point of view of its materiality, the relationships people have with it and the domestic spaces it moves through, it noted some of the features that may make it more likely that it is re-used to replace the purchase of other objects. These were summed up as properties of packs that are 'open' in two senses: they are physically up to the job of re-use and they can be rendered symbolically neutral enough for people to attach their own meanings to them. The chapter showed that design can enhance this openness as well as making it easy for people to integrate re-use into the spaces of their homes. This can mean simple features that make it easy to store packs without them taking up a great deal of space in a twilight zone or making it easy to remove labels and printing so that people can easily convert them from commodities into new objects or re-usable material.

The chapter introduced a range of examples of people re-using packs, either treating them as objects that can simply be used again for a similar purpose to their original one or as material out of which to make an entirely new object. This 'up-cycling' of the material of packaging, using it as raw material for new products, seems to fit more easily with commercial, or at least professional, approaches to packaging re-use. The ways that packaging is re-used by people untrained in design, and outside a business plan, are somewhat different. These re-uses seem to be more diverse, are often highly inventive, are close to the needs that everyday life throws up and often show less apparent concern for the appearance of the result. The difference between re-uses of packaging material designed by professionals and ones that emerge from the experience of inventive people in everyday life are evident through the ways they are represented in virtual spaces. The former are more visually coherent, sometimes conforming to the professionals' expectation that their work will be formally ground-breaking in the spirit of the tradition of the avant- garde. The latter are formally more casual, but their ground–up origin, and the vigour of the online communication that goes on between the people who originate them, may mean that they are a vanguard of another sort.

These seem to be re-uses that emerge genuinely from the ways people relate to packaging in everyday life, and the chapter briefly reviewed an approach to thinking about the diverse elements of these relationships together, as aspects of 'practices'. This approach can encompass the material, human and spatial aspects of re-use that the earlier chapters introduced, as well as ways that the more radical examples of re-use evident online might fold back into mainstream design and consumption. Taking up this latter point, an approach to 'designing together' that uses online networks to dissolve the boundary between production and consumption is likely to be able to capitalize on this indigenous inventiveness.

Notes

1   The effect of such non-material properties of objects on our willingness to be associated with them is taken by some psychologists to be evidence for a human propensity to be influenced by belief. Bruce Hood (2009) demonstrates this with reference to the unwillingness people demonstrate to be associated with an object that they think has been the possession of a murderer.

2   In an equivalent way, all objects are in principle open to personal meanings. A person's possessions may acquire a significant and unique meaning for them that derives from their biography, as in the perfume bottle discussed in Chapter 4. While such packaging is functioning as part of the extended self, and may be more likely to do so because of the type of object that it is, connected to self-presentation and relationships, its re-use has no significant environmental impact, because it does not replace another item. It does, though, demonstrate the potential for packaging to be thoroughly appropriated by its owner, facilitated by the engaging qualities of its design.

3   The success of the Doy Bags discussed above might appear to contradict this claim – it is the engaging colourful graphics from the packs from which they are made that give them their charm and make them attractive – but they are a different case for two reasons. Firstly the bags are themselves commodities which will need to be integrated into their owner's domestic 'moral economy', although this integration does not require that their user works any physical transformation on them; secondly, the packaging they are made of has already been up-cycled to make them into a saleable item.

4   The Instructables website is at www.instructables.com.

5   The Instructables website contains sets of instructions called instructables.

6   See, for instance, http://twinksplacenow.blogspot.com/search/label/Perpetual%20Blooms.

7   The ManyOne up-cycling community is at www.manyone.net/upcycling/.

8   People who have these attitudes fit the population segments 'Positive Greens' and 'Concerned Consumers' in Defra's environmental behaviour segmentation model (2008) discussed in Chapter 3.

9   The frameworks exist to develop and impose such standardization and have led to the successful development of CEN and ISO standards for some industrial packaging that have directly increased its re-use (Defra, 2009, p32).

6

Conclusion

The subject of packaging re-use may summon up slightly nostalgic images: children collecting empty lemonade bottles to be refilled, or the milkman in a 1950s film making his way down the path of a suburban house with empties clinking in his crate. Central to these images are packs for milk and lemonade that were designed *for* re-use. They were embedded in systems for production, packaging, distribution and consumption, with built-in features intended to influence people's behaviour to promote the re-use of the packaging involved. Milk bottles had 'please rinse and return' embossed on them; lemonade bottles carried a small deposit that was an incentive to return them. Both were robust enough to stand a number of journeys. But for the UK at least, these images smack of another era, when closed loops of re-use fit with shorter packaging supply chains and a doorstep delivery system, both of which have been overtaken by developments in the retailing of food and drink. They are images that do not fit with our times, character-ized as they are by an assumption of diverse choice for consumers who are mobile, the standardization of packaging for long supply chains and the rule of disposability, all of this supported in consumers' minds by the idea that we can dispose of packaging with a clear conscience if we recycle it.

Re-usable packs and the systems which generated them had re-use behaviour inscribed in them by their design. They were 'scripted' for re-use. Madeleine Akrich (1992, p208) suggests that such 'scripting' is a 'large part of the work of innovators', and design can do this scripting. It can specify the material and technical aspects of objects to strongly influence, if not deter-mine, how people relate to them in specific settings. Indeed, to be able to do this is a large part of design's claim to commercial relevance in encouraging people to buy products. It is only possible to 'script' packaging for re-use if this goes along with fundamental changes to the design of the systems that provide consumers with goods. The economic power of food producers and retailers is sufficiently strong to influence the frameworks that regulate them. Consequently, although UK government and industry have collaborated in response to European legislation to make advances in lessening the environ-mental impact of packaging through design, regulating packaging design and delivery systems to promote its re-use meets vigorous resistance if it conflicts with the economies of scale that are advantageous to producers and retailers. Such regulation is therefore currently politically unfeasible in the UK, even though possible in principle and in operation in many other parts of the world. Regulation for re-use conflicts directly with the UK Government's prevailing approach to environmental problems, which largely adopts interventions that are sympathetic to the ideology of the free market and work with producers through cooperation rather than legislation. Although detailed recent research has demonstrated the feasibility of such regulations[1] (Darlow/SISTech, 2002), and they operate elsewhere in Europe to standardize containers for re-use and offset higher costs by targeted taxation, schemes to promote closed-loop re-use are unlikely to be established in the UK any time soon.

This book has been a response to this situation. In the knowledge that top-down approaches to packaging re-use are unlikely, it has looked to the only other source of action: consumers themselves. It has demonstrated that, despite the grip of corporate interests on the possibility of promoting changes in the system of provision to promote re-use, the spontaneous actions of consumers provide glimmers of hope. The title of the book implies that it is possible to design for re-use now, and it is, but only in the niches and gaps that exist between our assumptions about what packaging is and the practices of everyday life that are exposed by the inventiveness that puts packaging to uses that subvert the intentions of designers and manufacturers and is facilitated and developed by the power of online communication. It may be possible for niche manufacturers to play on this inventiveness, but only by using fully the leverage that consumers' creativity and networked communication can give when they are combined. Innocent's approach to packaging is a tantalizing example of a formula that could be developed into something really effective were it fully integrated into an appropriate online network.

How to promote re-use in the meagre scraps of territory that exist within the prevailing system of provision remains a design problem – but it is a problem that requires designing that will work with the re-use practices that this book has exposed and punch above its weight from this constrained platform. Design propositions need to facilitate communication between inventive people about good ideas as much as they need to provide new types of packaging object. Design interventions need to work with the ways that people spontaneously subvert the assumption that packaging is waste, to more firmly embed revised practices of consumption that promote re-use. The preceding chapters show that people do re-use packaging as part of everyday practices. Re-use does take place. Design can help to make it more significant by working in full consciousness of the relationship between objects and practices and with an ethic of promoting sustainability. As Elizabeth Shove put it:

> If material artefacts configure (rather than simply meet) what consumers and users experience as needs and desires, those who give them shape and form are perhaps uniquely implicated in the transformation and persistence of social practice. (Shove et al, 2005, p4)

Our conventional approach to designing packaging – as if it had no connection to aspects of individuals' lives other than their actions as consumers – works to entrench the prevailing assumption that packaging is disposable, is incipient waste. Rather than helping this consumption practice to persist, design can contribute to its transformation. Madeleine Akrich notes the way that once a technology is established, it appears to be natural – it seems as if it could never have worked any other way than how it does; it becomes part of common sense. Her studies of the processes by which new technologies become established identify the negotiation that goes on between objects and the people who encounter and use them; their designs can play out in many different ways. Objects can be relatively 'obdurate' or more 'plastic' (1992, p207), in other words the script they embody can be, to a degree, 'open', in which case it leaves room for a consumer/user to ignore or subvert it, or it can be more 'closed', in which case there is no alternative for the consumer/user but to comply with it.[2]

Like any designed object, packaging can be more or less 'open' in this respect, and it seems from the examples in the previous chapters that, for some types of re-use, the more open packaging is, the more likely it is to be material for people's inventiveness. And it can be designed to be open – this quality can be kept in mind in its design alongside the ways in which it may fit into the practices of everyday life. As Kennedy and Krogman put it, to encourage less wasteful consumption patterns, 'we must examine social practices and the agents who practise them and design intermediary systems of provision' (2008, p183).

Packaging designs can be intermediaries in such 'intermediary systems'; they can be made so they not only interlock with the existing supply chain, but also provide openings for people to re-use them. In combination with the creativity and inventiveness of individuals, they can work with the parallel, emergent system of provision that this book has identified, which uses the leftovers, scraps and discards from consumption *themselves* as raw material. Clearly, though, this sort of indigenous re-use is unlikely to bring significant environmental benefits compared to those claimed for closed-loop packaging re-use systems. So why is it worth considering, apart from the fact that it is the only avenue open to promoting re-use in the UK? Three reasons suggest themselves.

First, re-use stands to enhance people's sense of their place in the world and may therefore have a positive influence on their wellbeing. Increases in conventional consumption do not seem to go along with increases in well-being (Jackson, 2005), but people seem to get satisfaction from mastering the material world – through being able to produce as well as consume. A connection between re-use and a sense of wellbeing is evident in a good deal of the online discourse that surrounds it and seems to be a feature of craft activities generally. Psychological benefit has been proposed for working with materials in an educational context (Sigman, 2008), and everyday crafts, in contrast to 'studio crafts' associated with galleries, have also been argued to bring psychological benefit by virtue of the absorbing processes they involve and the control over material that they afford (Fisher and Gibbon, 1997). The creative re-use identified in this book is a type of productive consumption, but it goes beyond the production of ensembles of objects that Colin Campbell names 'craft consumption' (2005). However, the opportunities it provides for self-expression may be as significant.

In the moral economy of the home it is not just meanings that circulate – we also engage with the materiality of packaging in domesticating it. The physical engagement involved in this process, the attachment to an ephemeral object that re-use achieves, also seems to be significant for people's sense of themselves, and hence perhaps for their psychological wellbeing. The need to be able to 'neutralize' packaging before it can be re-used, to remove labels to make it possible to imprint something of the self onto what are thoroughly commodified goods, seems to be an important part of turning these commodities into possessions. These are not simply things (briefly) owned, they are things manipulated, re-created, made again in a new form through craft processes. That such transformations occur even with these most ephemeral objects demonstrates the potency of everyday practices to transform manufactured goods that lack an intimate connection with the personality of their owners into possessions (Carrier, 1990, p582, Kopytoff, 1988).

Second, the online exchange of information about re-use does more than show that many varieties of re-use take place, that people are inventive with packaging and that they get satisfaction from re-using it, though it does all these. It also implies that this subversive relationship to conventional consumption could be a lever for bringing about more generalized change towards more sustainable practices. Globally distributed networks bring committed packaging re-users together with people who have advanced technical knowledge in a setting that values and promotes playful inventiveness. It is not possible to quantify the power that these networks have to amplify the efforts of individuals by the sharing and commentary they make possible. However, the energy that they display, and the fact that they seem to capture something of the equivocal relationship to conventional consumption that many people have and make something productive out of it, suggests that they could be a significant element in making it possible to change our practices with packaging.

The online communication surrounding packaging re-use involves sharing a particular sort of knowledge, which functions as a form of social capital. For some individuals, this capital may be cashed in by simply displaying a certain ethical credibility through communicating about their inventive re-use online. For others, among them perhaps the team that runs Instructables, sharing information about re-use may demonstrate a commitment to a more fundamental realignment of our relationship with commodities. Whatever the motivation of their contributors, the online networks that were set out in Chapter

5 comprise knowledge held in common as part of everyday life, articulated with, but independent of, the systems that provide goods and with which we interact as consumers. The fact that this knowledge is a collective resource, shared rather than sold, demonstrates this fundamental separation between re-use and the conventional commodity chain and the implicit resistance it represents to the system of provision.

The third way in which the re-use discussed in this book is significant comes out of a combination of the first two: people are motivated to re-use for the benefits it brings them as individuals, and they are able and willing to communicate about this online, sharing their knowledge and ideas. In isolation these facts are interesting, but in combination they may provide the basis for a design process that has the potential to affect the system of provision from the bottom up. The inventiveness with packaging described in Chapter 5, distributed online and between individuals, is potentially a form of design leadership. This is not the leadership of the 'early adopter', nor of the 'user innovator', because the objects that result from re-use are not simply adopted or used and modified but created – they have a new function; they are not necessarily born out of the use for which they were designed, but out of inventiveness, out of re-use.

However, this invention interlocks with the system of provision, because it depends on it. With relatively minor modifications to the way that manufacturers and retailers interact with their customers, invention such as this could feed back into the system of provision. This inventiveness is market-friendly in that it grows out of consumers' actions – for a company to recognize its potential could be another way of listening to the 'voice of the customer' (Griffin and Hauser, 1993). But it is more than that too – re-use offers us the prospect of revising people's relationship to packaging through a channel of communication that is more than just a feedback loop from customer to manufacturer: it comprises the customer demonstrating to the manufacturer the potential for packaging to fit with the practices of their everyday lives in ways that are necessarily unknown until they are discovered and which are therefore inaccessible to conventional marketing research. This creativity has features in common with the consumer innovation that has been a feature of the computer games industry, as well as software development through 'open source' software (Lerner and Tirole, 2002) and the convention of 'beta-testing' new software designs with users (Jeppeson and Molin, 2003).

Re-use, shared and collectively developed, could comprise a particular type of feedback loop to influence the re-design of the conventional relationship that people have to packaging. Relatively small modifications to packs, possibly only small alterations to specifications, could make big changes to re-use. The inventive online communities identified in Chapter 5 could lead this process, could show the way and be a platform for an engaged design process that feeds into and is fed by manufacturers and retailers and could influence policymakers. This mechanism for changing our relationship to packaging would not necessarily be based on campaigning to change attitudes and behaviour – though the element of re-use that derives from environmentalist dispositions could be reinforced through such campaigns. Instead, such a change would be based in the dissemination of revised practices with packaging that can fold back into manufacturing and affect the system of provision through the feedback loop between re-users and manufacturers that can be facilitated by online communication. Manufacturers could participate in this online dissemination, they could influence it or could set up more formal, product-specific feedback and communication loops for creative re-use. This would mean design for re-use by designing with re-use.

Notes

1   The environmental implications of closed-loop re-use are not clearly established, which may also contribute to the lack of commitment to them in the context of a market-orientated approach to the environmental implications of packaging. The packaging industry suggests there is no life-cycle benefit to container re-use, but its adoption in other countries suggests that this view ignores other benefits that accrue from it, but which do not affect industry, such as cutting the public cost of waste management and disposal and increasing employment (Platt and Rowe, 2002).
2   Bruno Latour (2000) describes just such a 'closed' script in his famous article about Berlin apartment keys: they are designed – 'scripted' – in such a way as to force the resident to lock the door after them.

References

Akrich, M. (1992) 'The de-scription of technical objects', in W. E. Bijker and J. Law (eds) *Shaping Technology/Building Society*, MIT Press, Cambridge, MA, pp205–224

Allwood, J. M., Laursen, S. E., de Rodriguez, C. M. and Bocken, N. M. P. (2006) *Well Dressed? The Present and Future Sustainability of Clothing and Textiles in the United Kingdom*, Institute for Manufacturing, University of Cambridge, Cambridge, UK

Andreasen, A. R. (2002) 'Marketing social change in the social change marketplace', *Journal of Public Policy and Marketing*, vol 21, no 1, pp3–13

Appert, N. (1811) *L'art de Conserver, Pendant Plusieurs Années, Toutes les Substances Animales et Végétales*, Patris et Cie, Paris

Arts Council England (2006) 'Own a piece of original art for 50p – Arts Council England and Sainsbury's launch artist-designed re-usable shopping bags', press release, 1 November 2006, www.artscouncil.org.uk/pressnews/press_detail.php?rid=1&id=738, accessed June 2007

Baren, M (1997) *How Household Names Began*, Michael O'Mara Books, London

Barthes, R. (1976) *Mythologies*, Paladin, London

Baudrillard, J. (1968) *The System of Objects*, Verso, London

Bayazit, N. (2004) 'Investigating design: Forty years of design research', *Design Issues*, vol 20, no 1, pp16–21

Belk, R. (1988) 'Possessions and the extended self', *The Journal of Consumer Research*, vol 15, no 2, pp139–168

Belk, R. (1995) *Collecting in a Consumer Society*, Routledge, London

Belk, R. (2006) 'Collectors and collecting', in C. Tilley, W. Keane, S. Kuchler, M. Rowlands and P. Spyer (eds) *The Handbook of Material Culture*, Sage Publications, London, pp534–546

Bell, B. and Wakeford, K. (eds) (2008) *Expanding Architecture: Design as Activism*, Distributed Art Publishers, New York

Bettison, P. (2007) 'Retailers pledge to cut carrier bags does not go far enough', press release, 28 February, http://new.lga.gov.uk/lga/core/page.do?pageId=41891, last accessed 20 November 2009

Beverland, M. B. (2005) 'Crafting brand authenticity: The case of luxury wines', *Journal of Management Studies*, vol 42, no 5, pp1003–1029

Bhatti, M. and Church, A. (2004) 'Home, the culture of nature and meanings of gardens in late modernity', *Housing Studies*, vol 19, no 1, pp37–81

Bickerstaffe, J. (2006) 'In praise of a hidden household hero', http://news.bbc.co.uk/1/hi/sci/tech/4836766.stm, last accessed 12 July 2007

Bijker, W. B. (1995) *Of Bicycles, Bakelites and Bulbs*, MIT Press, London

Blythe, M. A., Overbeeke, K., Monk, A. F. and Wright, P. C. (eds) (2003) *Funology: From Usability to Enjoyment*, Kluwer Academic Publishers, Dordrecht, The Netherlands, Boston, MA, and London

Bolam, F. (ed) (1965) *Paper Making: A General Account of Its History, Processes and Applications*, Technical Section of the British Paper and Board Makers' Association, London

Bourdieu, P. (1984) *Distinction: A Social Critique of the Judgement of Taste*, Routledge, London

Brown, J. (2008) 'Cellophane glamour', *Modernism/Modernity*, vol 15, no 4, pp605–626

Buchanan, R. (1992) 'Wicked problems in design thinking', *Design Issues*, vol 8, no 2, pp5–21

Buchanan, R. (2001) 'Human dignity and human rights: Thoughts on the principles of human-centred design', *Design Issues*, vol 17, no 3, pp35–39

Burke, C. and Grosvenor, I. (2003) *The School I'd Like: Children and Young People's Reflections on an Education for the 21st Century*, Routledge, London

Burke, C., Gallagher, C., Prosser, J. and Torrington. J. (2008) 'The view of the child: Explorations of the visual culture of the made environment', T. Inns (ed) *Designing for the 21st Century. Interdisciplinary Questions and Insights*, Ashgate, London

Butin, D. (2001) 'If this is resistance I would hate to see domination: Retrieving Michel Foucault's notion of resistance in educational research', *Educational Studies*, vol 32, no 2, pp157–176

Calinescu, M. (1987) *Five Faces of Modernity: Modernism, Avant-Garde, Decadence, Kitsch, Postmodernism*, Duke University Press, Durham, NC

Callon, M. (1987) 'Society in the making: The study of technology as a tool for sociological analysis', in W. E. Bijker, T. P. Hughes and T. J. Pinch (eds) *The Social Construction of Technological Systems: New Directions in the Sociology and History of Technology*, MIT Press, London

Campbell, C. (1992) 'The desire for the new: Its nature and social location as presented in theories of fashion and modern consumerism', in R. Silverstone and E. Hirsch (eds) *Consuming Technologies*, Routledge, London

Campbell, C. (2005) 'The craft consumer: Culture, craft and consumption in a postmodern society', *Journal of Consumer Culture*, vol 5, no 1, pp23–42

Carey, J. (1992) *The Intellectuals and the Masses*, Faber and Faber, London

Carrier, J. (1990) 'Reconciling commodities and personal relations in industrial society', *Theory and Society*, vol 19, no 5, pp579–598

Carson, R. (1963) *Silent Spring*, Hamish Hamilton, London

Chapman, J. (2005) *Emotionally Durable Design: Objects, Experiences and Empathy*, Earthscan, London

Charter, M., Peattie, K., Ottman, J. and Polonsky, M. J. (2002) *Marketing and Sustainability*, Centre for Business Relationships, Accountability, Sustainability and Society (BRASS), Cardiff

Cieraad, I. (2002) 'Out of my kitchen: Architecture, gender and domestic efficiency', *The Journal of Architecture*, vol 7, no 3, pp263–279

Clark, G. (1986) *Symbols of Excellence: Precious Materials as Expressions of Status*, CUP, London

Coley, N. G. (2005) 'The fight against food adulteration', *Education in Chemistry*, March, www.rsc.org/Education/EiC/issues/2005Mar/Thefightagainstfoodadulteration.asp

Corral-Verdugo, V. (1996) 'A structural model of reuse and recycling in Mexico', *Environment and Behaviour*, vol 28, no 5, pp665–696

Costall, A. (1995) 'Socialising affordances', *Theory and Psychology*, vol 5, no 4, pp467–481

Crouch, D. (1993) 'Representing ourselves in the landscape: Cultural meanings in everyday landscape', in R. B. Browne and R. J. Amprosetti (eds) *Continuities in Popular Culture: The Present in the Past and the Past in the Present and Future*, Bowling Green University Popular Press, Bowling Green, Ohio, pp26–48

Cwerner, S. B. and Metcalfe, A. (2003) 'Discourses and practices of order in the domestic world', *Journal of Design History*, vol 16, no 3, pp229–239

Dant, T. (1999) *Material Culture in the Social World: Values Activities, Lifestyles,* Open University Press, Milton Keynes

Dant, T. (2005) *Materiality and Society*, Open University, Milton Keynes, UK

Darlow, T. and SISTech (Scottish Institute of Sustainable Technology) (2002) 'Waste plans: Report on categorisation and pilot studies', Heriot-Watt University, Edinburgh, available at www.sistech.co.uk/media/EEPFinalReport_V2_.pdf

Darnton, A. (2008) 'An overview of behaviour change models and their uses', Government Social Research/University of Westminster, London, available at www.gsr.gov.uk/downloads/resources/behaviour_change_review/reference_report.pdf

Davis, F. (1992) *Fashion, Culture and Identity*, University of Chicago Press, Chicago, IL

De Certeau, M. (1984) *The Practice of Everyday Life*, University of California Press, London

Defra (2007a) 'Waste Strategy for England, Annex D', www.defra.gov.uk/ENVIRONMENT/WASTE/strategy/strategy07/pdf/waste07-annex-d.pdf, last accessed 12 January 2009

Defra (2007b) 'Report, questionnaire and data tables following Survey of Public Attitudes and Behaviours towards the Environment', www.defra.gov.uk/environment/statistics/pubatt/index.htm (accessed June 2009)

Defra (2008) 'A framework for pro-environmental behaviours', available at www.defra.gov.uk/evidence/social/behaviour/index.htm

Defra (2009) *Making the Most of Packaging: A Strategy for a Low Carbon Economy*, Department for Environment, Food and Rural Affairs, London

Desmet, P. M. A. and Hekkert, P. (2002) 'The basis of product emotions', in W. Green and P. Jordan (eds) *Pleasure with Products: Beyond Usability*, Taylor and Francis, London, pp60–68

DETR (2000) 'The plastic bag – A fashion accessory?', press release, 18 October

Dittmar, H. (1995) 'Objects, decision considerations and self-image in men's and women's impulse purchases', Harvester Wheatsheaf, Hemel Hempstead

Douglas, M. (1966) *Purity and Danger: An Analysis of the Concepts of Pollution and Taboo*, Routledge, London

Eisler, R. (2000) *Handbook of Chemical Risk Assessment: Health Hazards to Humans, Plants and Animals*, CRC Press, Boca Raton, FL

Fenichell, S. (1996) *Plastic: The Making of a Synthetic Century*, Harper Collins, London

Fisher, T. (2003) 'Plastics in contemporary consumption', unpublished PhD thesis, University of York, York

Fisher, T. (2004) 'What we touch touches us: Materials, affects and affordance', *Design Issues*, vol 20, no 4, pp20–31, available at http://mitpress.mit.edu/catalog/item/default.asp?ttype=6&tid=17205

Fisher, T. (2008a) 'Objects for peaceful disordering: Indigenous designs and practices of protest', *The Design Journal*, vol 11, no 3, pp221–238

Fisher, T. (2008b) 'Plastics in everyday life: Polymorphous (in-)authenticity', in B. Keneghan (ed) *Plastics: Looking at the Future and Learning from the Past*, Victoria and Albert Museum, London, pp144–151

Fisher, T. and Gibbon, J. (1999) 'The politics of craft', *Proceedings of the European Academy of Design Conference*, Sheffield, UK

Fisher, T., Hielscher, S. and Cooper, T., (2007) 'How often do you wash your hair? Design as disordering: everyday routines, human-object theories and sustainability', Seventh European Academy of Design Conference, Izmir, Turkey 10–13 April

Fisher, T., Wood, N. and Keyte, J. (2008) Hands on – Hands off: On hitting your thumb with a virtual hammer', in C. Rust, L-L. Chen, P. Ashtion and K. Friedman (eds) *Undisciplined! Proceedings of the Design Research Society Conference*, Sheffield Hallam University, Sheffield, UK

Forty, A. (1986) *Objects of Desire*, Thames and Hudson, London

Foucault, M. (1977) *Discipline and Punish: The Birth of the Prison*, trans Alan Sheridan, Peregrine Books, London

Francis, M. (1990) 'The everyday and the personal: Six garden stories', in M. Francis and R. T. Hester (eds) *The Meaning of Gardens*, MIT Press, Cambridge, MA, pp206–216

Francis, M. and R. T. Hester (eds) (1990) *The Meaning of Gardens*, MIT Press, Cambridge, MA

Franke, N. and Shah, S. S. (2003) 'How communities support innovative activities: An exploration of assistance and sharing among end-users', *Research Policy*, vol 32, no 1, pp157–178

Frederick, C. (1919) *Household Engineering: Scientific Management in the Home*, American School of Home Economics, Chicago, IL

Friedel, R. (1983) *Pioneer Plastic: The Making and Selling of Celluloid*, University of Wisconsin Press, Madison, WI

Gibson, J. J. (1977) 'The theory of affordances', in R. Shaw and J. Bransford (eds) *Perceiving, Acting and Knowing: Towards an Ecological Psychology*, John Wiley, London

Gibson, J. J. (1979) *The Ecological Approach to Visual Perception*, Houghton Mifflin, Boston, MA

Gloag, J. (1945) 'The influence of plastics on design', *Journal of the Royal Society of Arts*, vol 91, pp462–470

Goffman, E. (1951) 'Symbols of class status', *British Journal of Sociology*, vol 2, no 4, pp294–304

Goffman, E. (1990, 1959) *The Presentation of Self in Everyday Life*, Penguin Books, London

Gonzales, J. (1995) 'Autotopographies', in G. Brahm and M. Driscoll (eds) *Prosthetic Territories: Politics and Hypertechnologies*, Westview Press, Boulder, CO

Gordon, J. E. (1991) *The New Science of Strong Materials: Or Why You Don't Fall Through the Floor*, Penguin, Harmondworth, UK

Gosden, C. and Marshall, Y. (1999) 'The cultural biography of objects', *World Archaeology*, vol 31, no 2, pp169–178

Greenberg, C. (1939) 'Avant-garde and kitsch', *Partisan Review*, vol 6, no 5, pp34–49

Gregson, N. and Crewe, L. (2003) *Second-Hand Cultures*, Berg, Oxford

Gregson, N., Metcalfe, A. and Crewe, L. (2007a) 'Identity, mobility, and the throwaway society', *Environment and Planning D: Society and Space*, vol 25, no 4, pp682–700, also available at www.sheffield.ac.uk/content/1/c6/04/72/08/Identity%20Mobility%20 and%20the%20Throwaway%20Society.pdf

Gregson, N., Metcalfe, A. and Crewe, L. (2007b) 'Moving things along: The conduits and practices of divestment in consumption', *Transactions of the Institute of British Geographers*, vol 32, no 2, pp187–200

Griffin, A. and Hauser, J. R. (1993) 'The voice of the customer', *Marketing Science*, vol 12, no 1, pp1–27

Griffith, D. (1979) 'Decorative printed tins', Studio Vista, London

Gronow, J. (1997) *The Sociology of Taste*, Routledge, London

Gross, H. and Lane, N. (2007) 'Landscapes of the lifespan: Exploring accounts of own gardens and gardening', *Journal of Environmental Psychology*, vol 27, pp225–241

Hall, T. and Bannion, L. (2005) 'Co-operative design of children's interaction in museums: A case study in the Hunt Museum', *Co-Design*, vol 1, no 3, pp187–218

Harrod, T. (1995) *The Crafts in Britain in the 20th Century*, Yale University Press, New Haven, CT

Hastings, M. (1986) *Oxford Book of Military Anecdotes*, OUP, Oxford, UK

Hawkins, G. (2001) 'Plastic bags: Living with rubbish', *International Journal of Cultural Studies*, vol 4, no 1, pp5–23

Heft, H. (1989) 'Affordances and the body: An intentional analysis of Gibson's ecological approach to visual perception', *Journal for the Theory of Social Behaviour*, vol 19, no 1, pp1–29

Hendrick, I. (1942) 'Instinct and the ego during infancy', *Psychoanalytic Quarterly*, vol 11, pp33–57

Hirschmann, E. C. and Holbrook, M. (1982) 'Hedonic consumption: Emerging concepts, methods and propositions', *Journal of Marketing*, vol 46, pp92–101

Holbrook, M. (1996) 'Romanticism, introspection and the roots of experiential consumption: Morris the Epicurean', in R. Belk, A. Venkatesh and N. Dholakia (eds) *Consumption and Marketing: Macro Dimensions*, South Western College Publishing, Cincinatti, OH

Hood, B. (2009) *Supersense*, Constable and Robinson, London

Hooper, B. (1932) *Virgins in Cellophane: From Maker to Consumer Untouched by Human Hand*, Montgomery Flagg, New York

Imai, K., Nonaka, I. and Takeuchi, H. (1985) 'Managing the new product development process: How Japanese companies learn and unlearn', in K. B. Clark, R. H. Hayes and C. Lorenz (eds) *The Uneasy Alliance*, Harvard Business School, Boston, MA

Incpen (The Industry Council for Packaging and the Environment) (1997) 'Consumer attitudes to packaging', available at www.incpen.org/pages/data/Consumerattitudestopackagingsurvey.pdf, last accessed May 2008

Ingold, T. (2007) 'Materials against materiality', *Archaeological Dialogues*, vol 14, no 1, pp1–16

International Centre of Photography (1990) *Man Ray in Fashion*, International Centre of Photography, New York

Irish EPA (2004) Ireland's Environment 2004 State of the Environment, www.epa.ie/downloads/pubs/other/indicators/soe2004/

Irish Government Citizens' Information Resource (2009) *Plastic Bag Environmental Levy*, www.citizensinformation.ie/categories/environment/waste-management-and-recycling/plastic_bag_environmental_levy

Jackson, T. (2005) 'Living better by consuming less? Is there a "double dividend" in sustainable consumption', *Journal of Industrial Ecology*, vol 9, pp19–36

Jaworski, B. and Kohli, A. K. (2006) 'Co-creating the voice of the customer', in R. F. Lusch and S. L. Vargo (eds) *The Service-Dominant Logic of Marketing: Dialog, Debate and Directions*, M. E. Sharpe, Armonk, NY, pp109–117

Jeppeson, L.B. and Molin, M. (2003) 'Consumers as co-developers: Learning and innovation outside the firm', *Technology Analysis and Strategic Management*, vol 15, no 3, pp363–383

Jordan, P. W. (1997) 'The four pleasures – Taking human factors beyond usability', *Proceedings of the 13th Triennial Congress of the International Ergonomics Association, Tampere, Finland*, vol 2, pp150–152, The Finnish Institute for Occupational Health, Helsinki

Kaplan, R. and Kaplan, S. (1990) 'Restorative experience: The healing power of nearby nature', in M. Francis and R. T. Hester (eds) *The Meaning of Gardens*, MIT Press,

Cambridge, MA, pp238–243

Katz, S. (1978) *Plastics Designs and Materials*, Studio Vista, London

Katz, S. (1984) *Classic Plastics: From Bakelite to High Tech*, Thames and Hudson, London

Kennedy, E. H. and Krogman, N. (2008) 'Towards a sociology of consumerism', *International Journal of Sustainable Society*, vol 1, no 2, pp172–189

Klimchuk, M. R. and Krasovec, S. A. (2006) *Packaging Design: Successful Product Branding from Concept to Shelf*, John Wiley and Sons, Hoboken, NJ

Kopytoff, I. (1988) 'The cultural biography of things: Commodification as a process', in A. Appadurai (ed) *The Social Life of Things*, Cambridge University Press, Cambridge, UK, pp64–94

Kotler, P. and Lee, N. R. (2008) *Social Marketing: Influencing Behaviours for Good* (third edition), Sage Publications, London

Kubberod, E. (2005) 'Not just a matter of taste: Disgust in the food domain', unpublished PhD thesis, Norwegian School of Management, Oslo

Latour, B. (1992) 'Where are the missing masses? The sociology of a few mundane artefacts', in W. E. Bijker and J. Law (eds) *Shaping Technology/Building Society*, MIT Press, London, pp225–259

Latour, B. (2000) 'The Berlin Key: Or how to do words with things', in P. M. Graves-Brown (ed) *Matter Materiality and Modern Culture*, Routledge, London, pp10–21

Laurel, B. (ed) (2003) *Design Research: Methods and Perspectives*, MIT Press, Cambridge, MA

Lerner, J. and Tirole, J. (2002) 'Some simple economics of open source', *Journal of Industrial Economics*, vol 50, pp197–234

Lucas, G. (2002) 'Disposability and dispossession in the twentieth century', *Journal of Material Culture*, vol 7, no 1, pp5–22

Lupton, D. (1998) *The Emotional Self*, Sage, London

Lupton, E. and Miller, A. J. (1992) *The Bathroom, the Kitchen and the Aesthetics of Waste (A Process of Elimination)*, Kiosk, New York

Luthje, C., Herstatt, C. and Von Hippel, E. (2005) 'User-innovators and "local information": The case of mountain biking', *Research Policy*, vol 34, pp951–965

Macfarlane, A. and Martin, G. (2004) 'Beyond the ivory tower: A world of glass', *Science*, vol 305, no 5689, pp1407–1408

MacNaghten, P. and Urry, J. (2000) 'Bodies of nature: Introduction', *Body and Society*, vol 6, nos 3–4, pp1–11

Marks and Spencer (2008) 'How We Do Business Report 2008', available at http://corporate.marksandspencer.com/documents/publications/2008/2008_hwdb_report.pdf

McDonough, W. and Braungart, M. (2002) *Cradle to Cradle: Remaking the Way We Make Things*, North Point Press, New York

Meikle, J. L. (1995) *American Plastic: A Cultural History*, Rutgers University Press, New Brunswick, NJ

Minchinton, W. W. (1957) *The British Tinplate Industry: A History*, OUP, Oxford, UK

Misa, T. J. (1992) 'Constructing closure in technological change: Constructing "steel"', in W. E. Bijker and J. Law (eds) *Shaping Technology/Building Society*, MIT Press, London

Molotch, H. (2003) *Where Stuff Comes From: How Toasters, Toilets, Cars, Computers and Many Other Things Come To Be As They Are*, Routledge, London

Mugge, R. (2008) *Emotional Bonding with Products. Investigating Product Attachment from a Design Perspective*, VDM Publishing, Saarbrucken

Mugge, R., Schoormans, J.P.L. de Lange, A. (2007) 'Consumers' appreciation of product personalization', in G. Fitzsimons and V. Morwitz (eds) *Advances in Consumer Research*, Volume 34, Association for Consumer Research, Duluth, MN, pp339–341

Mugge, R., Schoormans, J. and Schifferstein, H. (2009) 'Incorporating consumers in the design of their own products. The dimensions of product personalisation', *Co-Design*, vol 5, no 2, pp79–97

Mustienes, C. and Baraton, I. (eds) (2000) *1000 Extra/Ordinary Objects*, Taschen, Cologne

Nora, P. (1989) 'Between memory and history: Les lieux de memoire', *Representations*, vol 26, pp7–24

Norman, D. (1990) *The design of everyday things*, Doubleday, New York

Norman, D. (1999) *The Invisible Computer: Why Good Products Can Fail, the Personal Computer is So Complex, and Information Appliances are the Solution*, MIT Press, Cambridge, MA

Packaging News (2006) 'Netto opts for unbranded bags to promote reuse', 1 August 2006, available at www.packagingnews.co.uk/news/637488/Netto-opts-unbranded-bags-promote-reuse/, accessed April 2008

Parliament of South Australia (2005) *Plastic Bags: Fifty Third Report of the Environment, Resources and Development Committee*, available at: www.parliament.sa.gov.au/NR/rdonlyres/4718FD62-3817-40CF-8B2B-0166D7420BC5/2324/53reportplasticbags.pdf

Parliament of South Wales Environment, Resources and Development Committee (2005) 'Plastic bags', paper tabled in the House of Assembly and ordered to be published, 5 April

Pawley, M. (1975) *Garbage Housing*, Architectural Press, London

Pinto, E. H. (1968) *Treen and Other Wooden Byegones: An Encyclopaedia and Social History*, Bell and Sons Ltd, London

Planet Ark (2002) *Irish Tax on Shopping Bags Nets 3.5 million Euros*, www.planetark.com/dailynewsstory.cfm?newsid=17404&newsdate=22-Aug-2002 (last accessed 14 November 2007)

'Plastes' (1941) *Plastics in Industry*, Chapman and Hall, London

Platt, B. and Rowe, D. (2002) 'Reduce, reuse, refill!', Institute for Local Self Reliance, Washington, DC, available at www.grrn.org/beverage/refillables/refill_report.pdf

Postrel, V. (2003) *The Substance of Style: How the Rise of Aesthetic Value Is Remaking Commerce, Culture, and Consciousness*, Harper Collins, London

Press, M. and Cooper, R. (2003) *The Design Experience*, Ashgate, London

Pro-Carton (2008) 'Carton packaging fact file', available at www.procarton.com/files/fact_file_3.pdf, accessed January 2009

Rankin, P. W. (2007) 'Metals: Packaging reuse and the need for a definition of industrial packaging', California Integrated Waste Management Board, www.ciwmb.ca.gov/Packaging/Metal/define.htm, last accessed 14 November 2007

Reckwitz, A. (2002) 'Towards a theory of social practices: A development in culturalist theorizing', *European Journal of Social Theory*, vol 5, no 2, pp243–263

Rehm, G. (2007) 'How to build a tin can waveguide WiFi antenna', www.turnpoint.net/wireless/cantennahowto.html, accessed July 2008

Riesman, D. with Denney, R. and Glazer, N. (1950) *The Lonely Crowd*, Yale University Press, New Haven, CT

Rith, C. and Dubberly, H. (2007) 'Why Horst W. J. Rittel matters', *Design Issues*, vol 23, no 1, pp72–91, available at www.dubberly.com/wp-content/uploads/2008/06/ddo_article_rittel.pdf

Rittel, H. and Webber, M. (1973) 'Dilemmas in a general theory of planning', *Policy Sciences*, vol 4, pp155–169

Rogers, H. (2005) *Gone Tomorrow: The Hidden Life of Garbage*, The New Press, New York

Ross, D. (2007) 'Backstage with the knowledge boys and girls: Goffman and distributed agency in an organic online community', *Organization Studies*, vol 28, pp307 –325

Rozin, P. and Nemeroff, C. (1990) 'The laws of sympathetic magic: A psychological analysis of similarity and contagion', in J. W. Stigler (ed) *Cultural Psychology*, CUP, Cambridge, UK

Sainsbury's (2007) www.j-sainsbury.co.uk/files/reports/cr2007/index.asp?pageid=72, last accessed 14 November 2007

Scanlan, J. (2005) *On Garbage*, Reaktion Books, London

Schiffer, M. B. (1999) *The Material Life of Human Beings: Artefacts, Behaviour and Communication*, Routledge, London

Schuler, D. and Namioka, A. (eds) (1993) *Participatory Design: Principles and Practices*, Lawrence Earlbaum Associates, Mahwah, NJ

Shaw, B. (1993) 'Formal and informal networks in the UK medical equipment industry', *Technovation*, vol 13, no 6, pp349–365

Shaw, B. (1998) 'Innovation and new product development in the UK medical equipment industry', *International Journal of Technology Management*, vol 15, nos 3–5, pp433–455

Shipton, J. (2007) 'Understanding the secondary functions of packaging: UK domestic reuse', unpublished PhD thesis, Sheffield Hallam University, Sheffield, UK

Shove, E. (2003) *Comfort, Cleanliness and Convenience: The Social Organisation of Normality*, Berg, Oxford, UK

Shove, E. (2006) 'A manifesto for practice oriented product design', document presented at the Designing and Consuming Workshop, Durham, UK, 6–7 July

Shove, E. and Warde, A. (1997) 'Noticing inconspicuous consumption', www.lancs.ac.uk/fass/sociology/esf/inconspicuous.htm, accessed 8 December 2005

Shove, E., Watson, M. and Ingram, J. (2005) 'The value of design and the design of value', *Joining Forces, International Conference on Design Research*, University of Art and Design, Helsinki, 22–25 September

Shove, E., Watson, M. Hand, M and Ingram, J. (2007) *The Design of Everyday Life (Cultures of Consumption)*, Berg, Oxford

Sigman, A. (2008) *Practically Minded: The Benefits and Mechanisms Associated with a Craft-Based Curriculum*, Ruskin Mill Educational Trust, Nailsworth, Gloucestershire

Silverstone, R., Hirsch, E. and Morley, D. (1992) 'Information and communication technologies and the moral economy of the household', in R. Silverstone and E. Hirsch (eds) *Consuming Technologies: Media and Information in Domestic Spaces*, Routledge, London

Soroka, W. (1996) *Fundamentals of Packaging Technology*, The Institute of Packaging, Sherbourne, Dorset

Strasser, S. (1999) *Waste and Want, A Social History of Trash*, Metropolitan Books, New York

Taylor, C. (1989) *Sources of the Self*, Cambridge University Press, Cambridge, UK

Thompson, M. (1979) *Rubbish Theory: The Creation and Destruction of Value*, Oxford University Press, Oxford, UK

Tilley, C. (2007) 'Materiality in materials', *Archaeological Dialogues*, vol 14, no 1, pp16–20

Tomes, N. (1999) *The Gospel of Germs: Men, Women and the Microbe in American Life*, Harvard University Press, Harvard, MA

Twede, D. (1998) *Packaging Materials*, Pira International, London

Urban, G. L. and Von Hippel, E. (1988) 'Lead user analyses for the development of new industrial products', *Management Science*, vol 34, no 5, pp569–582

Von Hippel, E. (1986) 'Lead users: A source of novel product concepts', *Management Science*, vol 32, no 7, pp791–805

Von Hippel, E. (1988) *The Sources of Innovation*, Oxford University Press, Oxford, UK

Von Hippel, E. (2005) *Democratizing Innovation*, MIT Press, London

Wallendorf, M. and Arnould, J. E. (1988) 'My favourite things: A cross-cultural inquiry into object attachment, possessiveness, and social linkage', *Journal of Consumer Research*, vol 14, pp531–541

Walter, D. (2005) *De-junk Your Mind: Simple Solutions for Positive Living*, Penguin, London

Walter, D. and Franks, M. (2003) *The Life-Laundry: How to De-junk Your Life*, BBC Books, London

Woodward, S. (2007) *Why Women Wear What they Wear*, OUP, Oxford, UK

WRAP (2009) 'New figures show single use carrier bags cut by 48%', press release, 17 July, www.wrap.org.uk/wrap_corporate/news/new_figures_show.html, accessed 17 July 2009

Yarsley, V. E. and Couzens, E. G. (1942) *Plastics*, Penguin, Harmondsworth, UK

Index